W9-ADT-815

ABSTRACT ART

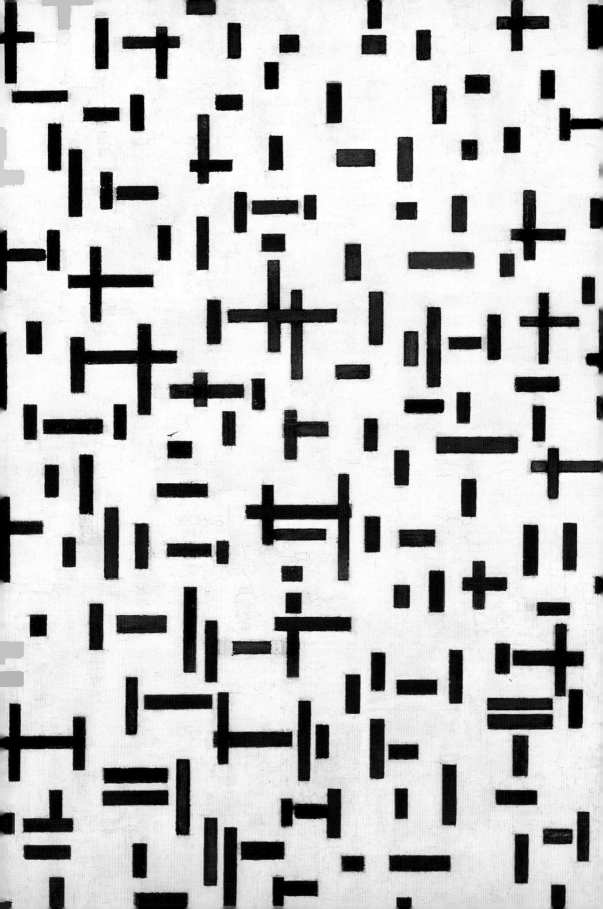

ABSTRACT ART

MEL GOODING

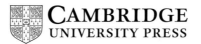

CAMBRIDGE
UNIVERSITY PRESS

PUBLISHED BY THE PRESS SYNDICATE OF THE
UNIVERSITY OF CAMBRIDGE
The Pitt Building, Trumpington Street, Cambridge
United Kingdom

CAMBRIDGE UNIVERSITY PRESS
The Edinburgh Building, Cambridge CB2 2RU, United Kingdom
40 West 20th Street, New York, NY 10011-4211, USA
10 Stamford Road, Oakleigh, Melbourne, 3166, Australia
Ruiz de Alarćon 13, 28014 Madrid, Spain
Dock House, The Waterfront, Cape Town 8001, South Africa

http://www.cambridge.org

First published by Tate Publishing, a division of Tate Enterprises
Ltd, London 2001

Cover designed by Slatter-Anderson, London
Book designed by Isambard Thomas
Typefaces Monotype Centaur (9/10.5 pt)
and Adobe Franklin Gothic
System (Apple Macintosh) [IT]

Printed in Hong Kong by South Sea International Press Ltd

A catalogue record for this book is available from the British Library

Library of Congress Cataloguing-in-Publication Data is available.

Measurements are given in centimetres, height before width,
followed by inches in brackets

Cover:
František Kupka
Amorpha: Fugue in Two Colours 1912 (detail of fig.11)

Frontispiece:
Piet Mondrian
Composition in Black and White 1917 (detail of fig.15)

ISBN 0 521 00631 7 (paperback)
ISBN 0 521 80928 2 (hardback)

Contents

ABSTRACTION: AN INTRODUCTION

NEW WAYS TO STATE WHAT IS THE CASE

All art is abstract, in the sense that all art engages with the world and abstracts aspects of it in order to present us with an object or an event that enlivens or enlightens our apprehension of it. 'The world is everything that is the case', wrote Ludwig Wittgenstein at the outset of a life-long philosophical project that began with an effort to describe the world logically and ended with reflections on the problematic nature of the very language that we must use if we are to describe anything at all. The progress of art from representation to abstraction in some ways paralleled that quintessential modern quest for a new kind of truth. 'Everything that is the case' includes nature and society, the built environment, the structures of religion, art and science, and all the marvellous and mundane acts, thoughts and emotions, speculations and imaginings that comprise a complex human culture. From the early years of the twentieth century painters and sculptors in the European traditions of art, more than at any time since the Renaissance, consciously sought radically new ways to represent their experience of that world. They set out to create an art that would reveal aspects of reality that seemed inaccessible to the techniques and conventions of figurative art.

The great and enduring idea that painting and sculpture could picture the reality of the world by means of an illuminating imitation (*mimesis*), or through the illusionistic representation of natural phenomena, was suddenly brought into question. Figurative representation was seen by many artists as a limitation upon their capacity to represent the actualities of experience, including spiritual experience, with the kind of intensity or clarity that would reveal its true nature. Artists felt the need to take account, moreover, of realities newly revealed by science, dynamics newly discovered by mathematics and physics, new ideas in psychology, and post-Darwinian developments in biology, in religion and what used to be called 'natural philosophy'. They were responsive also to the new politics of social democracy, of Communism and of individual freedom. They were aware of great changes in industrial technology, of the beginnings of manned flight, of the internal combustion engine, and of photography and film. The cities in which they lived were in a state of dynamic transformation. All this entailed the rejection of those old forms of art that sought to imitate the appearance of things, and the invention of new forms that would reveal the hidden relations between things. Objects are objects, they can be pictured; but to represent dynamic relations *between* objects required an abstract visual language.

It was not that artists at the beginning of the new century fully understood, in the way of theoreticians, scientists and other specialists, the multifarious intellectual, spiritual and technological developments that were taking place. They did not need to. Artists have their own work to do, their own kinds of intuitive research to undertake. It was, rather, that something very exciting was in the air, and that the word *new* applied to a great deal of what was happening. It was to become, with 'modern', one of the positive keywords of the century, a verbal talisman for artists and critics alike. This book will consider what a large number of very different twentieth-century artists, working in different places with different ideas and intentions, created in response to the great modernist injunction 'Make it new!'

For modern artists, creative originality was subject to the imperatives of authenticity: response to the demands of the inner life, truthful engagement with external reality, and directness of utterance. This emphasis upon individual experience made it inevitable that their work would take many different forms, and that what they thought about the meaning and purposes of art would be correspondingly diverse. There has been no 'abstract movement' as such, but many manifestations of a powerful trend in modern art away from the *representation* of recognisable objects in pictorial space (in whatever style or manner) and towards the *presentation* of a painting or a sculpture as a real object in real space. Some artists believed that such an object might actually emanate a kind of energy, sensuous or spiritual, activating the space around it. The disposition of lines, shapes and colours on the canvas, or of pure sculptural forms in space, having been abstracted from nature, now operated directly upon the spectator, as did the natural phenomena of light, colour, texture and movement. For some it was felt that the abstract work of art might induce a sense of the numinous or the transcendent, taking the place in spiritual life of the sacred objects or icons of the past.

All paintings and sculptures are, of course, 'real objects in real space', and abstract works must represent something or other to the mind, just as figurative works present an image to the eye. These distinctions are not intended as paradoxical wordplay, but to emphasise important differences of purpose and effect between the two kinds of art. They demonstrate the difficulties of terminology we all encounter when we talk or write about abstract art. These difficulties are compounded by the sometimes mystifying and contradictory language that characterises the statements and writings of many of the greatest abstract artists. What artists write is often very interesting in relation to the sources and intentions of their work, but it is never definitive or conclusive as to its effects. It is for the spectator to create meanings, not for the artist to dictate them.

Many artists responded to the unprecedented freedom of expression that was a necessary condition of abstraction by extending the expressive possibilities of figurative art. Arbitrary colour; vehement brushwork and exaggerated textures; collage and other disruptions of the surface; distortions of the figure and of other natural forms: these were among the diverse devices they adopted. In many cases what had previously been regarded as preliminary techniques, rough workings of materials *towards* completion and 'finish', came to be regarded as valid in their own right, as authentic expressive features of the finished work. One of the (many) problems that arise in any discussion of abstraction and its histories in modern art is that the term 'abstract' itself has been widely used to describe figurative distortion or exaggeration in painting and sculpture, or formal devices that depart from conventions of naturalistic representation. Works by Pablo Picasso, Henri Matisse, Constantin Brancusi and Henry Moore, among other great figurative artists, have often been described as 'abstract'. This common usage of the term was intended to indicate a shift away from the representation of objects or space as perceived in nature, from 'what things look like', towards a more generalised, simplified or distorted representation of them. In the light of my opening remark, this should not surprise us. *All* figurative art, including realistic academic painting and sculpture, is 'abstract' in terms of that first observation: it works by selection, emphasis, exaggeration.

In any case, we know perfectly well that the world does not actually look like its painted representations: even the most naturalistic devices, such as perspective, conventions of shade and tone, techniques of modelling and so on, merely create the illusion for the spectator of looking as through a window onto the world, or at something 'life-like', though inert, in space. Artists have always known that this magical transformation is a complex business, entailing elements of design and structure, line and shape, texture and facture, rhythm and interval, light and shadow, colour and tone. These components are *abstract*, in the sense that they are perceived properties and qualities of things, not the things themselves. Realising this profound truth about naturalistic representation with the force of revelation, many of the best artists of the twentieth century sought to liberate art from what has been called the 'tyranny of appearance', especially from academic conventions of illusionistic imitation, and from the deceiving devices that had been taught in art academies since the Renaissance.

NAMING 'THE NEW ART'

Once abstract art had departed, to a greater or lesser extent, from naturalistic description, its own history became complicated, as did the history of the term itself. There was no simple agreed description or definition. There came into being many modes of abstraction with different intentions and effects. 'Abstraction' had no fixed starting point in time or place, and from different premises it went in various directions, its trends diverging and converging, crossing and overlapping. Abstract artists have learnt from the diversities of decorative art, from architecture, from the beautiful structures of mathematics and geometry, from folk art and ethnographic objects, from the astounding discoveries of the invisible and recurrent structures of reality revealed by new photographic techniques, from the diverse insights of the new psychology, from the new technologies of the machine. Above all, music provided the example of a purely non-representational art with variations of formal structure and great affective power. This 'new art', abstraction, proved to be a potent means for the expression of a great diversity of experiences and ideas. Abstract artists created original imageries that match in intensity and power those of the great tradition of figurative art. Abstraction did not supersede representational art but took its place beside it, discovering new possibilities of vision, changing the way in which things are seen and known.

The first major exhibition to survey the various international tendencies towards an art that abandoned 'the imitation of natural appearance' was put on at the Museum of Modern Art, New York, in April 1936. According to Alfred H. Barr, the exhibition's selector and the author of its influential catalogue *Cubist and Abstract Art*, the 'pictorial conquest of the external visual world had been completed and refined many times and in different ways during the previous half millennium. The more adventurous and original artists had grown bored with the painting of facts.' The term 'abstract' was, he wrote, 'most frequently used to describe the more extreme effects of this impulse away from "nature"'.

We may feel that we know what Barr meant by 'the imitation of natural appearance', but very few abstract artists would admit to an 'impulse away from nature', indeed, quite the contrary! And what is 'the painting of facts'? Most abstract painters would claim that this was precisely what they were doing: that colour, for example, was a 'fact', and that lines, planes and textures were primarily 'facts', and only when combined in particular ways become something else, more difficult to describe. Barr acknowledged that the term 'abstract' was inexact. He rejected the alternatives, 'non-objective' and 'non-figurative', on somewhat literal (if not disingenuous) grounds: 'the image of a square is as much an "object" or a "figure" as the image of a face or a landscape; in fact, figure is the very prefix used by geometers in naming A or B the abstractions with which they deal.' It is easy to see that the abstract figures of geometers serve a quite different purpose from those of painters; the term 'figurative' applied to paintings refers to the *pictorial* figuring of things perceived and identified in the natural world. Attempting to argue his case logically, Barr succeeded only in creating terminological confusion. As its title indicates, his great pioneering exposition (exhibition and book together) included much work that was not yet purely 'abstract' but which was intended to demonstrate the routes taken by painting towards abstraction.

The idea of 'abstraction' and 'abstract art' thus presented problems of definition from the outset. The terms rejected by Barr continued to be used, along with others, and there is nothing we can do about it. They are usually identified with specific historical circumstances: Guillaume Apollinaire, the early champion of Cubism, invented the phrase 'pure painting'; 'Suprematism' was a neologism coined by Kasimir Malevich in 1915 to identify his own abstract work and that of others closely connected with him; 'the non-objective world' was the title of a book Malevich published in 1926; *De Stijl* (Dutch for 'The Style') was the title of a magazine founded in 1917 to promote the ideas of a group of like-minded artists, architects and typographers; Piet Mondrian described his own style as Neo-Plasticism; in the early 1930s a Paris-based international group organised itself around an annual review entitled *Abstraction-Création*; at about the same time certain 'Constructivist' artists tried, unsuccessfully, to replace the adjective 'abstract' with its opposite, 'concrete'; the French critic Michel Tapié invented the term *tachisme* for a kind of painting created out of numerous painterly strokes (French: *taches*); 'action painting' and Abstract Expressionism were terms freely applied to the work of American painters of quite different styles and intentions; and so on. Most histories of abstract art are structured around these stylistic developments and divisions, and the terms associated with them.

Although this book is roughly historical in its approach, it is not an account of that kind. Its emphasis is upon abstract paintings and sculptures as objects having a history of their own, and susceptible to diversities of personal 'reading'. Abstract art gives the spectator an unprecedented freedom of imaginative response, but this is not to say that an abstract painting or sculpture can mean anything at all. As Roland Barthes has observed: 'one does not create meanings in just any way, (if you doubt that, try it): what controls the critic is not the meaning of the work, it is the meaning of what he writes about it.' Discussion in this book of the individual works and their contexts is, then, simply *exemplary*. There is little room for the elaboration of the critical or historical complexities that attend upon the abstract work of art as it takes its place in a discourse in which the possibilities of meaning are 'controlled' but never exhausted. The viewer who sees a work in isolation, as simply the occasion of sensuous experience, will miss a great deal, as will the viewer who reads an 'explanatory' text and registers the work merely as an example of a historical or personal 'style', or an item from an 'ism'.

For the purposes of this book the problem of definition is resolved simply. By *figurative* art I mean any mode of representation in painting and sculpture that offers the eye the illusion of a perceived reality, however simplified, distorted, exaggerated or heightened. *Abstract* is art is not thus figurative. Whatever other terms may have been used in whatever historical, ideological, or critical circumstances, I shall nominate as 'abstract' any art that has that negative quality. No account of abstract art can ignore the importance to its development of certain kinds of figurative art (most notably Cubism) that come close to abstraction. We shall find that the key to meaning in art, which is resemblance, applies to abstraction no less than to figuration, but that resemblance may be more than a matter of what things 'look like': a concept, for example, may find resemblance in an object.

Abstract art, even more than representational art, demands the actual encounter, the sensation of the thing itself. It depends for its effects, whether they are simple or complex, sensuous or conceptual, upon the presence of the viewer, who brings possibilities of meaning to its presentations of forms and colours, its visible patterns and rhythms, its forms, shapes and textures. Meanings are created as these concrete actualities impinge, through the senses, upon the receiving imagination. It is in the discourse around art that words come into play: spoken or written, language answers to image, articulating personal responses that enable the negotiation of shared aspects of meaning. Thus, my descriptions and analyses of the works illustrated in this book have no authority beyond that granted by the reader as reasonable in relation to his or her own responses to those works or others like them. Abstract art has many ways of touching upon things known, but its reference to events in familiar narratives is never literal and unequivocal: it always demands imaginative extrapolation. This book traces the themes of this introduction in relation to some of the most significant manifestations of this new art of the twentieth century. It will serve its critical purpose if the reader encounters the real thing with an enhanced sense of its potentialities of meaning and its powers of expression.

I

ABSTRACTION AND THE INVISIBLE

MALEVICH AND THE ROYAL INFANT

A black square. Not quite regular, slightly tilted. Pitch black, its bituminous surface badly crackled: the most famous blank in the history of modern art. Confronted with Malevich's *Black Suprematist Square* 1914–15 (fig.1), you ask the crucial question: what am I to make of this image? And that begs another: in what sense is this an *image* at all? Other questions will follow, insistently, for it is in the very nature of looking at and thinking about abstract works of art that such questions arise. Abstract art denies many of those possibilities of interpretation offered by figurative images; it demands instead an effort of the imagination, a creative response. What will help us to answer those questions, to make that constructive response? Firstly, we must be prepared to look without preconceptions or prejudice, to break with habits of expectation, to respond directly to the dynamic relations between its visible elements of colour and form. Secondly, we must look to the relations between this work and others in that living discourse of art, between artists, and between artists and their public, that takes place across generations, backwards and forwards in time. We need to look; we need to know something; and we need to imagine.

Much is known about this painting of a black square and about the conditions of its making. We have the words of Malevich, its creator, to suggest ways of looking at it, and a great deal is known about the intellectual and creative ferment out of which this seminal work, this ending and beginning of painting, emerged in late 1914 or early 1915. It is very nearly the first absolutely

1
Kazimir Malevich

Black Suprematist Square 1914–15

Oil on canvas
79.6 × 79.5
(31¼ × 31¼)
Tretyakov, Moscow

abstract painting, the first painting that seems to refer to nothing but itself, that derives from nothing but its near-geometric forms, that is nothing but what it is: a black square on a white ground; a black square within a white square. It is a mysterious object. We may wonder, at first sight, why this object has created such inordinate interest, why so many histories of the art of the twentieth century attach so much importance to it. Prompting reflection, it begins its work in the imagination.

To begin with we may see it as a void, a dark empty space. Alternatively, we may see it as an image of the ultimate fullness, the black into which everything

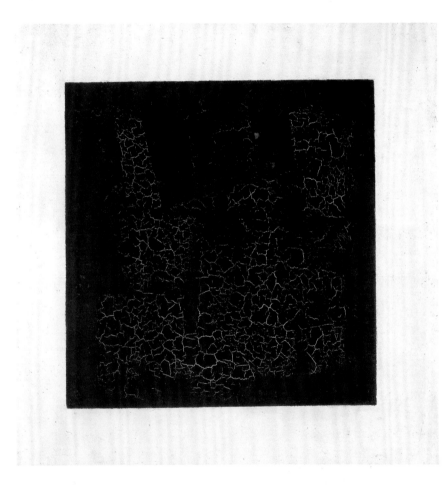

is dissolved or gathered, the distilled precipitation of matter itself, the white around it appearing to be space and light. It is, then, an image that may be seen to contain its opposite. Either way, it is not a picture of an object or objects in the world as seen in the light of common day. An area of black paint framed by white on a canvas support, it is an object in its own right. It clearly functions in ways quite different from a figurative painting. Absolutely simple, it works by reduction, elimination and concentration. (As we shall see, its circumstantial origins imply that it is an image of eclipse.) It is confrontational, demanding an active response rather than a passive reception. It is an object for contemplation, but not of the kind we might bring to a still life, a landscape, a portrait or a narrative picture.

The painting reproduced here is the earliest version. In the collection of the Tretyakov Gallery in Moscow, it is too fragile to travel. The strange irregularities of the *craquelure* correspond to the configuration of the coloured geometric shapes of an earlier composition hidden by the black square, triumphantly obliterated by its superimposition. We witness in this the dramatic moment of Malevich's great discovery. The black, so decisively applied, deteriorated so quickly that Malevich repainted the square in the early 1920s using a paint incompatible with the first layer, leading to the extreme instability of its surface. He went on to paint many versions of the black square, indicating that the image-object had a potential independent of its various realisations: it was a sign that could be repeated. It had first appeared in

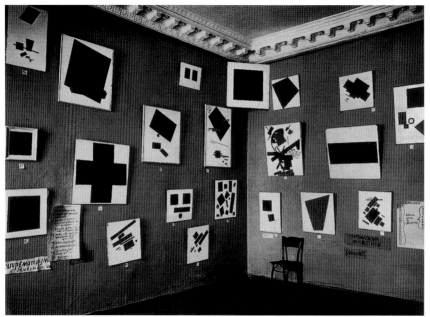

2

Photograph showing the *0.10 (Zero.Ten)* exhibition, December 1915

Malevich's work, not as a painting at all, but as an element in designs for the backdrop and costumes of a Futuristic opera, *Victory over the Sun*, on which he had worked in 1913 with his close friends, the composer Mikhail Matiushin and the poet Alexei Kruchenykh. In a letter to Matiushin in May 1915, enclosing one of the original drawings, Malevich wrote: 'The curtain depicts a black square, the germ of all potential, [which] acquires awesome force as it develops. It is the father of the cube and the sphere. Its disintegration will elevate painting astoundingly.' He was at this time secretly engaged on his first completely abstract paintings, the so-called 'Suprematist' works, first seen at an extraordinary group exhibition, *The Last Futurist Exhibition of Pictures 0.10 (Zero.Ten)*, in December of that year in St Petersburg (fig.2).

In an astonishing moment of intuition Malevich had seen in that image the energetic origin for a wholly new way of painting. He had realised its mythic potential as a painted sign for a new beginning, the signifying progenitor of any number of created forms whose dynamic relations would take place in the imagined space of the painting rather than the imaginary space of a picture. Denying these shapes the pictorial illusion of three dimensions, he at once banished from his Suprematist paintings the recessive space and modelled forms of post-Renaissance representation, the naturalistic light and colour of Impressionism, and the Cubists' fleeting glimpses of the objective world. It was what could *not* be seen that mattered: the energy within things, that higher order of connectivity between phenomena, invisible but ever-present in the perceptible world, the abstract *spiritual* energy that animates the universe, independent of the objects through which it moves. The purpose of Suprematism was to picture or present this 'non-objective world', to take the researches of Paul Cézanne, Picasso, Georges Braque, Matisse and Fernand Léger, and of the Russian and Italian Futurists, to their logical – or supra-logical – conclusions. It aimed to do so in the creation of 'painting as such', painting freed from naturalistic conventions and from the inconsequential disciplines of specialised craftsmanship.

In his manifesto, 'FROM CUBISM TO FUTURISM TO SUPREMATISM: THE NEW REALISM IN PAINTING', published to coincide with the 1915 exhibition, Malevich declared:

I have transformed myself in the zero of form and fished myself out of the rubbishy slough of Academic art. I have destroyed the circle of the horizon and escaped from the circle of objects, the horizon-ring that has imprisoned the artist and the forms of nature. The square is not a subconscious form. It is the creation of intuitive reason. The face of the new art. The square is the living, royal infant. It is the first step of pure creation in art.

This kind of high-flown rhetoric, poetic, contradictory and stridently nonsensical, using common words in uncommon ways, characterises much of the writing of the Russian avant garde. In language that provocatively rejects academic banalities, but has many of the qualities of the higher nonsense, it announces the absolute newness of the work it promotes. From 1910 Malevich had been at the centre of Russian artistic experiment: his paintings had drawn on native Russian sources (folk art, popular graphics, icons), combining them with a succession of Western stylistic influences, above all, that of Cubism. Many of the greatest early Cubist paintings of Picasso and outstanding works by Cézanne, Matisse and André Derain were familiar to the young leaders of the new Russian art, who saw them, banked floor to ceiling, in the Moscow salons of the great businessmen-collectors, Sergei Shchukin and Ivan Morosov, opened to the public on Saturday afternoons. It is also difficult to underestimate the importance of Malevich's associations with the brilliant younger generation of Futurist writers, musicians and artists. These included the intellectual composer-painter-theorist Matiushin; the mercurial Kruchenykh, who called for an abstract poetry of 'the word and the letter *as such*', inventing a language beyond syntactical logic and everyday sense; the great experimental poets Velimir Khlebnikov and Vladimir Mayakovsky; and the artists Mikhail Larionov, Natalia Goncharova and Olga Rozanova.

Malevich was also deeply influenced by the Russian mystic-mathematician

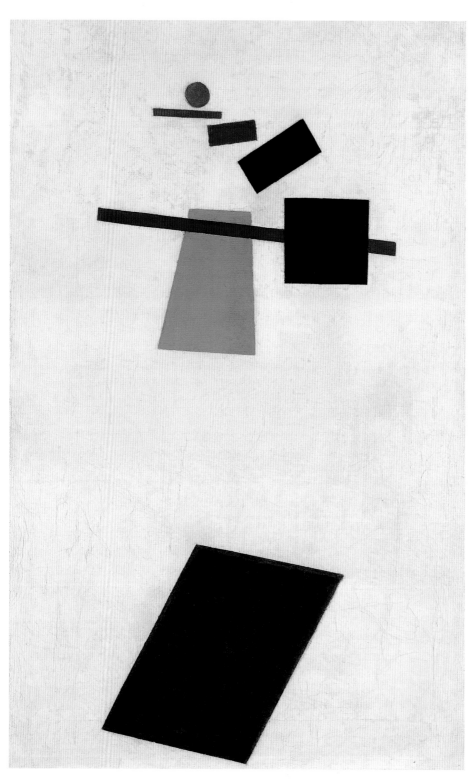

3
Kazimir Malevich

Suprematism: Painterly Realism of a Football Player (Colour Masses of the Fourth Dimension) 1915

Oil on canvas
70 × 44
(27½ × 17⅜)
Stedelijk Museum, Amsterdam

4
Kazimir Malevich

Red Square: Painterly Realism of a Peasant Woman in Two Dimensions 1915

Oil on canvas
53 × 53
(20⅞ × 20⅞)
Russian State Museum, Leningrad

P.D. Ouspensky, who wrote of a 'fourth dimension' beyond the three to which our ordinary senses have access, the invisible reality of which extended beyond the conventional geometry of line, plane and volume. These quasi-scientific ideas were used by many artists (not only in Russia) to provide a poetic alternative to the literalism of perspectival description and its positivist validation of the circumscribed material world, the finite, imprisoning 'circle of objects … the horizon ring'. We encounter the black square, in this account, as the two-dimensional 'visible' face not merely of a cube, but of an imagined multi-dimensional form in cosmic space. Painting becomes a kind of intuitive metaphysics, intimating another dimension of reality, accessible only to the imagination, made visible only by art. Malevich's description of his new style as 'Suprematism: The New Painterly Realism' asserts its superiority to all previous styles in its representation of this 'reality'. In his influential book *Tertium Organum* 1912 Ouspensky had written:

'There is no aspect of life that does not reveal to us an infinity of the new and the unexpected if we approach it with the *knowledge* that it is not exhausted by its visible aspect, that behind the visible there lies a whole world of the invisible, a world of comprehensible forces and relations beyond our present comprehension. The *knowledge* of the existence of the invisible world is the first key to it.'

We do not need to believe in the metaphysics of the fourth dimension, or in Malevich's often far-fetched and fantastic claims for his work, in order to find Suprematist paintings beautiful and moving, any more than it is necessary to subscribe to Christian beliefs in order to appreciate and be moved by an explicitly Christian art. The solemn, deadpan literalism of his titles – *Suprematism: Painterly Realism of a Football Player (Colour Masses of the Fourth Dimension)* 1915 (fig.3), for example, or *Red Square: Painterly Realism of a Peasant Woman in Two Dimensions* 1915 (fig.4) (both of which works are entirely abstract) – may provoke a smile; their implicit reverence for the ordinary person is, nevertheless, affecting. Our deeper response will depend upon how seriously we take Malevich, not on whether we share his beliefs and ideas: it requires that subtle kind of ironic distance that Samuel Taylor Coleridge described as 'the willing suspension of disbelief'. It is a matter of fact that we will base our judgement upon the ways in which we find the work entering our own consciousness and modifying our own feelings and thoughts. In this respect, our response to the *Black Suprematist Square* may be akin to our response to a Byzantine icon. Profoundly influential on the way in which Malevich and other Russian modernists looked at and thought about art, icon painting was also 'suprematist' in its concern with the absolute rather than the circumstantial, with space and time beyond the immediate, with things beyond the visible. The icon is a *sign*, not a representation: its figurative elements are conventional significations rather than portraits of an earthly being, and its space is a cosmic, two-dimensional, unchanging gold, a sign for an infinite spiritual reality that cannot be pictured.

Olga Rozanova's extraordinary *Untitled (Green Stripe)* 1917 (fig.5) has just that elemental iconic power of direct presentation. Its subtitle was probably added later, as a simple means to identification, for what we see is not so much a stripe (which is a two-dimensional figure: colour bounded by two edges) as the image of a beam of light, a pillar of green fire. And just as the edges of this green vertical shimmer into the pale space it divides, so does it have no end or beginning, being implicitly infinitely continuous above and below the edge of the canvas. Similarly, in *Non-Objective Composition (Suprematism)* c.1916 (fig.6), the horizontal and vertical bars of colour, their powerful frontal presentation emphatically hieratic, shine forth from an infinity of black and seem to extend into an endless space beyond their visible termination at the canvas edge. As radical as anything by Malevich, and quite different, Rozanova's paintings propose, just as surely as his, novel possibilities for painting and a novel kind of spirituality for art. They are a new kind of icon, freed of any religious orthodoxy, but marvellously suggestive of a space and time beyond the immediate.

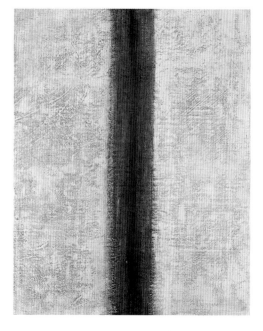

Green Stripe, unknown in the West until the great exhibitions in the early 1980s of his collection, was the very painting that set the young George Costakis off on his epic quest for neglected works of the Russian avant garde. He came across it in a Moscow studio in 1946: 'Up to this time I had known only the Cubist paintings of Picasso, and assumed everything in that vein must be in brown or black. I was dazzled by the flaming colours of this unknown work, so unlike anything I had seen before.' We now know that there were several other single-'stripe' paintings – green, yellow and pink – hidden in Russian museum basements at that time. Although the work of Malevich was, until the 1980s, little seen by Western artists (and mostly through black and white reproductions), over the years since Barr's references to it in the widely circulated catalogue of the 1936 MOMA show, the 'black square' had become legendary. Rozanova's work was unseen altogether, and has only recently begun to enter the consciousness of Western artists. The history of the creative and critical reception of abstract art is more complex than might be suggested by stylistic description, by remarking the dates of its creation or by the retrospective chronological tracing of movements, precedents and 'influences'.

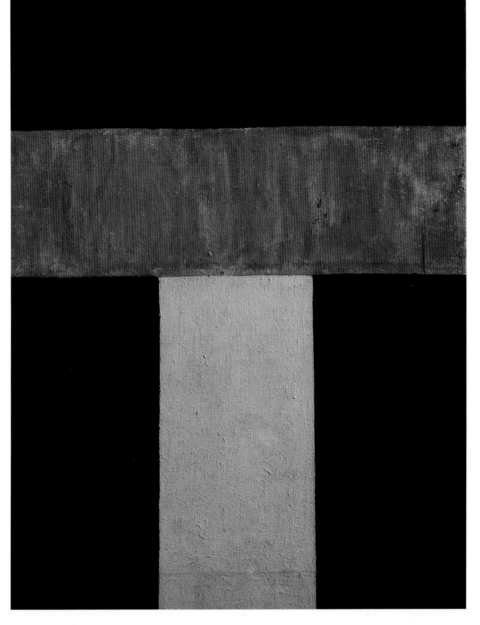

5
Olga Rozanova

Untitled (Green Stripe)
1917

Oil on canvas
71.5 × 49 (28⅛ × 19¼)
Rostov Kremlin

6
Olga Rozanova

*Non-Objective
Composition
(Suprematism) c.*1916

Oil on canvas
57.5 × 44 (22⅝ × 17⅜)
Russian State Museum,
Leningrad

KANDINSKY AND THE PIANO WITH MANY STRINGS

The vivid, formless colour and the strange, linear near-figuration of Wassily Kandinsky's *Improvisation No.19* 1911 (fig.7) is something very different from the hieratic simplicity and near-geometric drama of Suprematist painting. Here, we are presented with a chromatic and tonal richness: a rough arc of scarlet, yellow, orange, crimson, green and white, dissolving rightwards and downwards into a mess of vibrant violets, purples and blues, pale to dark. Much of this lower-central passage is so quickly and lightly brush-scribbled that the light of the white-primed canvas shines through. The colour in this painting is that of the spectrum, as if the rainbow had been magically scattered to momentarily occupy the rectangle, a fugitive moment of light and energy, an atmospheric chaos. Its title seems to suggest that the work was made as a response to inner impulse, as a gifted pianist might spontaneously invent a piece of music with a particular mood in an appropriate key. 'Generally speaking,' Kandinsky wrote, 'colour is a power which directly influences the soul. Colour is the keyboard, the eyes are the hammers, the soul is the piano with many strings. The artist is the hand which plays, touching one key or another, to cause vibrations in the soul.'

This parallel of music and painting haunted Kandinsky, as it had many artists, composers and writers in the last years of the old century and the early years of the new. 'All art', wrote the English critic Walter Pater, 'aspires to the condition of music.' Music is the most purely abstract of the arts, beyond language, purely sensuous and yet capable of touching directly the spirit of the listener. In moving towards abstraction, visual art was aiming for this directness of access to the inner, spiritual reality of the spectator, seeking to become the outward and visible sign of an invisible truth. Charles Baudelaire, in a famous poem, had described *correspondances* between different sensory phenomena:

Like prolonged echoes that merge far away
In a dark and profound oneness
As vast as night, as vast as light,
Perfumes, sounds, colours answer to each other.

Behind this lies the idea that our different senses respond in an immediately contingent way to particular stimuli – tastes, sounds, colours – but are themselves components of a deeper structural aesthetic that recognises direct correspondences between disparate sensory experiences. Closely connected to this belief in synaesthesia is the idea that every sensation is at once an experience and a sign: that is to say, it is an aspect of a reality beyond the material immediacy of the visible, the tangible and the audible; and beyond words. Kandinsky called this spiritual reality, which transcends the sensible world and is beyond rational understanding, 'the soul'. Our most profound intimations of it are achieved through religion and art.

Kandinsky believed that painting, like music, should be expressive of the artist's 'inner life', the deepest intuitions and feelings, without recourse to 'the reproduction of natural phenomena'. Like music, it should devote itself to the creation of autonomous forms, and to the application of methods that are proper to its own media and free it from 'mere representation'. From this aspiration arose 'the modern desire for rhythm in painting, for mathematical, abstract construction, for repeated notes of colour, for setting colour in motion'; in short, for abstraction. During the years from 1910 to 1914, making paintings that he saw as corresponding to the forms of music (he distinguished between *Impressions, Improvisations* and *Compositions*), Kandinsky remained uncertain as to whether it was possible to make an art that excluded all reference to the natural world. On the one hand, colour is itself associative; on the other, purely abstract images might be 'merely decoration, which are suited to neckties and carpets'. He felt that it would take time for the public to be able

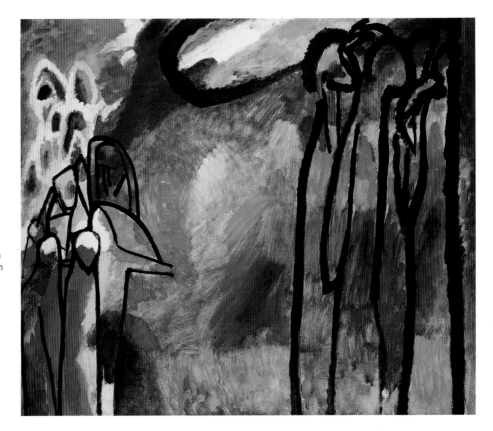

7
Wassily Kandinsky

Improvisation No.19
1911

Oil on canvas
120 × 141.5
(47¼ × 55¾)
Stadtische Galerie im
Lenbachhaus, Munich

to respond spiritually to 'the inner harmony of true colour and form composition'.

Looking again at *Improvisation No.19* we may be struck by the deep space created by those busy blues and purples ('like prolonged echoes that merge far away'); we may even see them as a visual analogy for a plangent musical chord (Kandinsky's alternative title for this painting was *Blue Sound*); we may be delighted in ways difficult to describe in words, as we are by music. We are also aware of mysterious transparent figures, like monkish *personnages*, to the right and lower left of the picture, and of the strange shapes, drawn in white, to the upper left, which may suggest the onion domes of an orthodox monastery or of Moscow's St Basil's Cathedral. These are what Kandinsky described as 'veiled' or 'concealed' forms, whose appeal was intended to be 'less to the eye and more to the soul'. These motifs (elongated human figures, horses and riders, hills and valleys, churches and castles, lances and cannons, rainbows and storm clouds) have subliminal associations with the revelatory purposes of the paintings of this period. Many of them have titles or subtitles — *The Deluge, The Last Judgment, All Saints* — that refer explicitly to prophetic and apocalyptic themes. Kandinsky's mysticism was partly Russian Orthodox in origin, partly

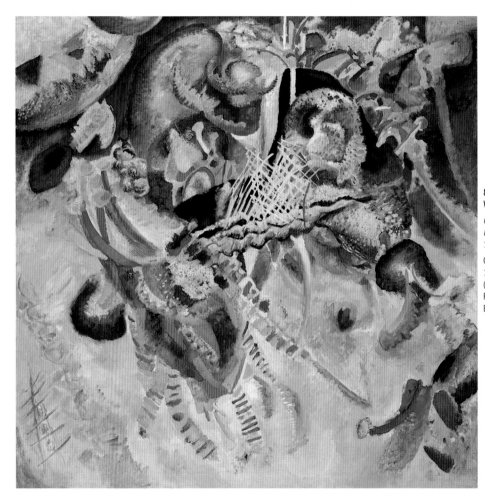

8
Wassily Kandinsky

Controlled Improvisation: Fugue
1914

Oil on canvas
129.5 × 129.5
(51 × 51)
Fondation Beyeler,
Basel

derived from the utopian teachings of the theosophist Rudolf Steiner — himself a painter, who believed art to be a powerful spiritual force — partly a matter of an inescapable personal predisposition. He was deeply committed to art as a means of revelation of new spiritual possibilities.

As the First World War approached and then overtook Europe like a cataclysm, Kandinsky's apocalyptic themes took on a new urgency, and acquired different possibilities of meaning. *Controlled Improvisation: Fugue* (fig.8) was painted in March 1914. The *Improvisations*, which numbered over thirty-five between 1909 and 1914, were the outcome, in Kandinsky's own words, of a 'largely unconscious, spontaneous expression of an inner impulse'. In *Fugue* we will not find a structural analogy with a strict musical form so much as random repetitions and a spiralling dynamic (characteristic of Kandinsky) that goes first clockwise, then anti-clockwise. The word 'fugue' here means 'flight', and this provides a cue to a response to the painting. Its shapes and colours can be seen as having freed themselves from their earthbound forms, and to have flown out into an ecstatic universe of pure relations. Stroke, line, smudge, stain, stipple, curve, criss-cross, swerve: narrative or scenario here can only be described in terms of paint itself, enacting its own drama. And then, as often happens in expressive abstraction, the eye at play within the welter of texture and colour begins to see analogies and resemblances: the tumult of a storm,

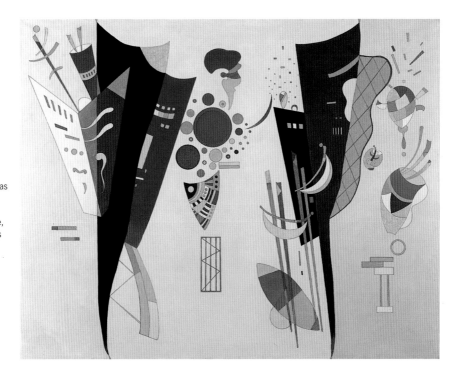

9
Wassily Kandinsky

Reciprocal Accord
1942

Mixed media on canvas
114 × 146
(44⅞ × 57½)
Musée D'Art Moderne,
Paris (Centre Georges
Pompidou)

wild weather, fireworks. Objects begin to separate themselves out: flowers, fruits, a dark hill, birds in flight, a ship at sea. And these in their turn dissolve again into pure colours and complex textures. The colour in *Fugue* is too gay, its over-all effect too musical, for our knowledge of its terrible historical context to over-determine our response to it. It might be seen as an attempt at transcendence, as representing a flight from physical existence and tragic contingency into another realm, where experience is not of the eye alone, but of the spirit. This is painting conceived not as a window on to the visible, but as a doorway to the ineffable, to experience beyond language. 'Thus', wrote Kandinsky, 'one should not approach art by means of reasoning and understanding, but through the soul, through experience.'

In Moscow during the Revolutionary period and after, Kandinsky was

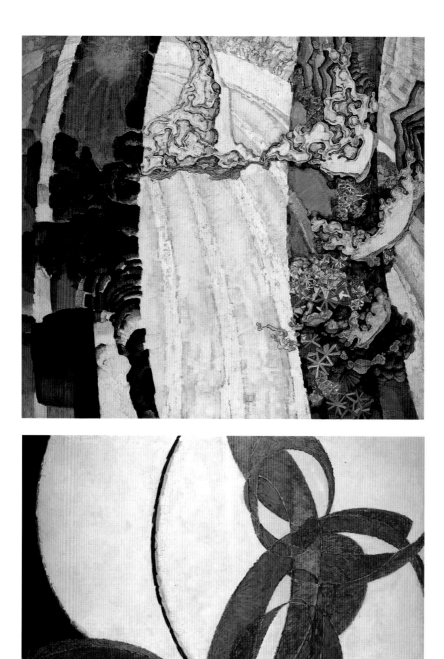

10
Franti šek Kupka

Cosmic Spring
1911–12

Oil on canvas
115 × 125
(45¼ × 49¼)
National Gallery,
Prague

11
Franti šek Kupka

Amorpha: Fugue in Two Colours 1912

Oil on canvas
211 × 220
(83⅛ × 86⅝)
National Gallery,
Prague

exposed to the powerful artistic personality and intensely spiritual charisma of Malevich, and he became deeply involved in the great art-educational experiments of the late 1910s in Russia. In the early 1920s he carried this pedagogic commitment to the Bauhaus in Weimar Germany. As he systematised his ideas on abstraction as a teacher and theorist, his painting became less improvisatory and free in its manner, his colour flatter, his forms more hard-edged and geometric. The painterly brush-mark he had regarded as directly expressive of the spirit gave way to the play of invented forms, both biomorphic and mechanical, in configurations analogous to the dynamically harmonic relations of things in the visible world. *Reciprocal Accord* 1942 (fig.9) is typical of his later style, in which principles very different to those that animated the abstract Expressionist paintings of 1910–14 are at work. 'This art creates alongside the real world a new world that has nothing to do externally with reality. It is subordinate internally to cosmic laws.' A painting is more than a picture of those forces that shape external reality and that make the world and the universe what it is; it is, rather, an *enactment* of them. In this respect, Kandinsky was consistent: as early as 1913 he had written: 'The creation of the work of art is the creation of the world.' The artist is an instrument of nature: the hand that plays the piano. This is an ancient idea and one that many abstract artists of the twentieth century have felt to be true.

One such, who had many affinities with Kandinsky, was the Czech, František Kupka. Following his own path, he had left Prague, first for Vienna and then for Paris, where he eventually fell into the brilliant company of modernist 'pure painters' inspired by the Cubism of Picasso and Braque. Kupka, however, was not so much interested in the dynamism of modern life, or in the natural phenomena of light and colour, as in colour and form as aspects of a mystical symbolism. Like Kandinsky, he conceived of painting as a kind of visual music, capable of presenting directly to the mind and spirit of the viewer the transcendental 'realities' of the cosmos, the metaphysics of creation itself. *Cosmic Spring* 1911–12 (fig.10), with its symphonic swelling of chromatic colour chords, is a stupendous image of 'the creation of the world'. *Amorpha: Fugue in Two Colours* 1912 (fig.11), as its title implies, is concerned with the invisible music of creation out of which forms emerge, imagining this as a contrapuntal arabesque of elemental contrasts, red and blue, black and white. Kupka, the mystic, was never interested in abstraction merely as a stylistic development: he believed, as did Kandinsky, that its purpose was revelation.

MONDRIAN AND BOOGIE WOOGIE

Piet Mondrian was a man whose austerely modest manner and style of life concealed a passionate temperament. His progression from an Expressionistic, Fauvist naturalism to the balanced calm and apparent simplicity of pure abstraction is that of a rigorously logical reduction of means and an elegant refinement of purpose. Paradoxically, these creative economies were the more rigorous for the power of the emotional necessity to which they answered. As with Malevich and Kandinsky, painting for Mondrian was a philosophical and spiritual activity. It was the means to the revelation of a reality hidden behind the forms of nature, and to the creation of a way of life that would ultimately

free the human spirit from tragic contingency and bring it to the peace and
beauty of perfect equilibrium. His ideas of spiritual (and by extension, artistic)
evolution were also influenced by the mystical doctrines of theosophy, which
held that humanity was progressing from the dualistic disharmonies of current
existence to rediscover a unity of being such as had existed in the prelapsarian
harmony. Mondrian believed that art had a vital part to play in this evolution.
It may be that these metaphysical and utopian considerations were a
sublimation of the violent intensity of his response to the natural world, and
an effort to allay the anxieties of spirit that this provoked in him. The
development of his work has a singular directness of purpose that reflects an
extraordinary clarity of thought and feeling, and an absolute dedication akin to
that of a mystic. Mondrian's intellectual and moral rigour is without question
related to the spiritual climate of his native Holland, with its Calvinist

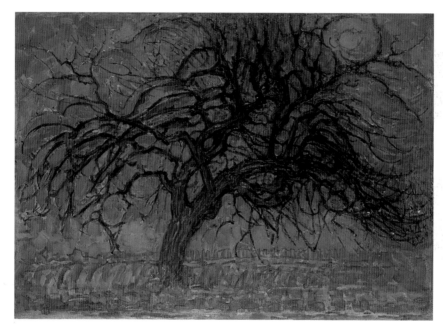

12
Piet Mondrian

The Red Tree 1908

Oil on canvas
70 × 99 (27½ × 39)
Gemeentemuseum, The
Hague

13
Piet Mondrian

*Oval Composition
(Trees)* 1913

Oil on canvas
94 × 78 (37 × 30¾)
Stedelijk Museum,
Amsterdam

emphases on predestination, grace by election, behavioural restraint, distrust of
extravagance, and the value of ethical speculation. At the level of construction,
these national predispositions are reflected in the ordered control of nature that
is a condition of the survival of the country itself. Holland's landscape is made
by man and dominated by the geometrics of straight line and right angle, the
horizontal and vertical.

Contemplating the painterly vehemence and chromatic colourism of *The Red
Tree* 1908 (fig.12), we will surely be reminded of Mondrian's great Dutch
predecessor, Vincent van Gogh. Mondrian was also aware of the work of the
Paris-based Fauves, led by Henri Matisse and André Derain, whose work was
characterised by non-naturalistic, decorative high colour and fervent
brushwork, and of Dutch artists who followed this trend. This is the work of
an artist excited by the extreme vitality of nature, who sees, like van Gogh, a

kind of fire in green and growing things. Hot blues and reds predominate, the latter changing from the orange of the individual jab-like strokes along the base, through the optically vibrant, flame-like, writhing strokes of scarlet, crimson and blue of the tree's trunk, to a duller red-brown at the tree's extremities. The visual effect of these transitions is of a centrifugal radiation upwards and outwards. This untended apple tree, proliferating and ramifying into tenuous twigs, is reverting to wildness; it presents an alarming image of lost control, of disequilibrium, of entropy. Its reductive and violent colour and its fantastic divaricate occupation of the canvas rectangle are aspects of a *symbolic* function. It is a vivid metaphor for the 'tragic' condition of contingent nature which it would be the function of a pure 'plastic' art to transcend. 'The

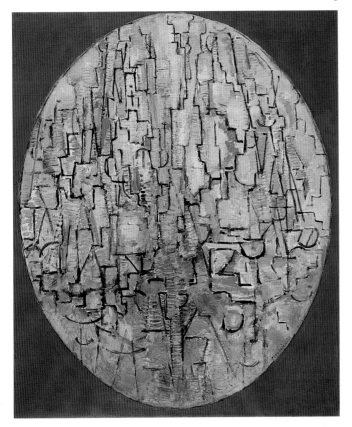

fantastic [the naturally capricious] is beautiful', says the 'naturalistic' painter in Mondrian's 'Essay in Triologue Form' of 1919. 'Beautiful but tragic', replies the 'abstract-real' painter (Mondrian himself); 'if you follow nature you will only in small measure abolish the tragic in your art. Naturalistic painting can make us *feel* the harmony that transcends the tragic, but it cannot *express* it determinately, since it does not express equilibrated *relationships* exclusively.'

Composition No. VI (Composition 9, Blue Façade) (fig.14), painted in Paris in 1914, marks a crucial moment in Mondrian's development of an abstract vision. A key motif of his work for many years had been trees, progressing from *The Red Tree* towards cooler, more schematic presentations, such as *Oval Composition (Trees)* 1913 (fig.13), that analysed rhythms of growth and organic structure in complex arrangements of curved lines. Now he turned to architectural structures, to the simple rectangular geometry of apartment buildings close to his studio in Montparnasse. *Blue Façade* was based on sketchbook drawings depicting an exposed inner wall of a demolished multi-storey building, a motif composed of vertical rectangles of colour. The oppositions of vertical/horizontal, straight line/plane became for Mondrian the essential formal means to a purely painterly expression of the spiritual equilibrium that he believed was the precondition of a new civilisation. He was perfectly explicit about this in his writings from 1917 onwards: painting provided a visual model of human relations in the future, it was an 'aesthetic expression of the new spirit', an intimation of utopian possibilities. In time,

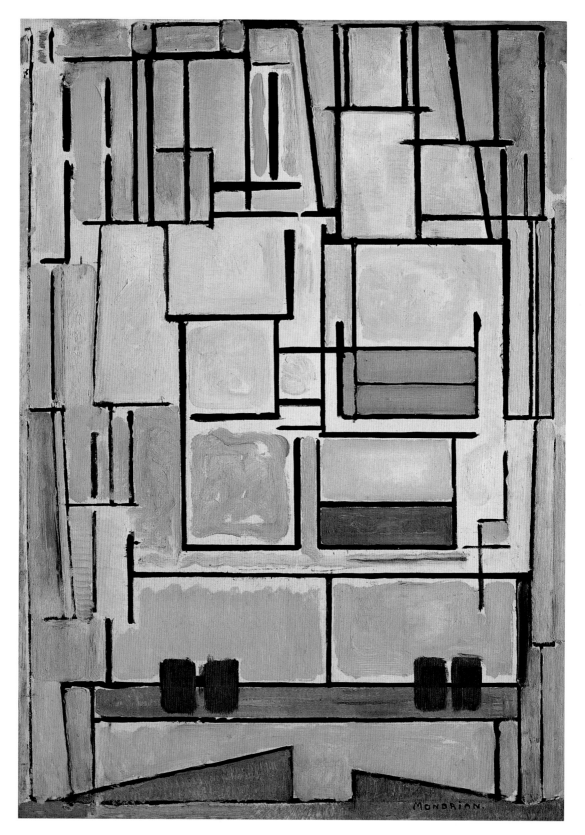

the qualities of 'abstract realism' would be transferred from art to life. 'When the new man has transformed nature in the image of what he himself will be – *nature and non-nature in equilibrium* – then mankind, including yourselves, will have regained paradise on earth!' This paradise sounds very like Holland.

Blue Façade is painted, however, in a way that suggests that the artist is still very much embroiled in the hectic actuality of the here and now. Its handling is extremely loose and free, at times almost perfunctory. The rectangles are in most cases incomplete, and the leakage of space between them sets up a visual agitation. They are in-filled with roughly gestural strokes, quickly laid down in one direction or another, down or across. Others betray a twist of the wrist, a swift change of direction or the quick application of two or three brushloads, each with a different gesture. The cloud of pale blue in the near-square enclosure at lower centre is executed in two distinct moves, a wrist-twisting scribble, followed by a decisive stroke from top left down to the right. To its left, the same blue has been lightly and roughly brushed over three black verticals. Two pairs of grey vertical strokes, applied quickly with a flat brush, have eliminated four still clearly visible black blocks (signs for fireplaces in the original sketch) rising from the horizontal grey-blue bar near the bottom. All of this suggests an urgency of execution, but reproduction flattens much of the painterly incident to suggest a considered, ordered composition. The painting is, in fact, anything but schematic; it has a sketchiness, an expressive *élan* at odds with its architectural structure.

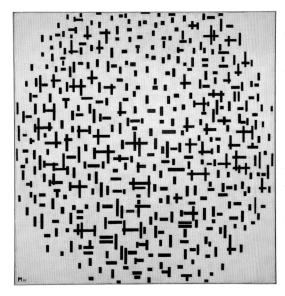

14
Piet Mondrian

*Composition No. VI
(Composition 9, Blue
Façade)* 1914

Oil on canvas
95.5 × 68
(37⅝ × 26¾)
Fondation Beyeler,
Basel

15
Piet Mondrian

Composition with Lines
1917

Oil on canvas
108 × 108
(42½ × 42½)
Kröller-Müller Museum,
Otterlo

After *Blue Façade* came the so-called 'plus and minus' paintings. Here, the schematic rendering of a pier (seen as if from above, simplified to a passage of vertical strokes from lower-centre to centre) and the surrounding sea (predominant horizontals intersected by shorter verticals) was ultimately reduced – in *Composition with Lines* 1917 (fig.15) – to an oval distribution of small, black, rectangular blocks (some intersecting) over an undifferentiated white ground. The visual effect of these paintings is of a restless, rhythmic, optical shimmer; of an oceanic cosmos ceaselessly busy around the barely discernible architectural vertical. It is an art of *perpetuum mobile* in which the eye finds no point of rest: in spite of the geometry of its components and of their configuration (rectangles in an oval) this is still painting 'as the expression of [changeable] things'.

The classic Mondrians of the 1920s and 1930s appear at first sight to have finally transcended the inner turbulence that is so strongly implied in earlier paintings. *Composition with Blue and Yellow* 1932 (fig.16) presents us with a set of formulaic oppositions: black line to white or colour plane; thick line to thinner lines; lines to edges; planes open to the canvas edge to planes enclosed; rectangular planes to the canvas square; chromatic colour to white. As with all Mondrian's works after 1921, it confines itself to primary colours – black, white and grey – its arrangements are asymmetrical, and its compositional relations are controlled within a strictly orthogonal structure, i.e. perpendicular with right angles ('orthogonal' combines the Greek for 'upright' and 'angle'). These purely vertical and horizontal rectilinear relations were seen by Mondrian as a visible 'expression of the unchangeable'; they are a metaphor for the invisible universal relations that lie beyond the 'capriciously' crooked and particular forms of nature. His post-1921 paintings combine vertical and horizontal lines and rectangular planes in configurations that imply an infinite number of possible variations, each as harmonious, as dynamically equilibrated, as the next. Like icons, and for corresponding reasons, each painting is the same but different: the reality they picture is unchanging. Mondrian is possibly the first modern artist to have invented a distinctive image-form that is at once definitive and susceptible to any number of discrete manifestations. It is an image of perfect harmony and repose, but it avoids the hierarchy of elements implied by the symmetry of a centralised image or by the sign of the cross. Its 'plastic' presentation of contrapuntal order makes visible the universal principle hidden by the everyday appearance of specific natural things, 'for the particular, which leads us away from the principle, is abolished by this procedure; the common factor remains. The expression of things gives way to the pure expression of relation.'

16
Piet Mondrian

Composition with Blue and Yellow 1932

Oil on canvas
55.5 × 55.5
(21¾ × 21¾)
Fondation Beyeler,
Basel

The relation of black lines and colour planes is clearly visible in reproductions of Mondrian's later paintings. Their design was intended by the artist to have something in common with the contrapuntal rhythms of modern dance and jazz – one painting is sub-titled *Foxtrot* and his last two works were entitled *Boogie Woogie* – a music in which the descriptive forms and subjective emotions of melody are destroyed. Other aspects of their actual material presence are not, however, so perceptible. Mondrian sought to eliminate the illusion of three-dimensional space created by the 'window' of the picture-frame by directly mounting his stretched canvases onto a white backboard, thus projecting them into real space as objects whose clearly defined right-angle edge implies the continuity of the black lines, and of the coloured or white planes, into the infinity of the circumambient space. No painter before him had used this simple device to propose the transcendence of the image over the material limitations of the support. Contemplating these image-objects in reality, however, complicates our response: we are touched by poignant accidents of material facture that have nothing to do with the idealism of the paintings' declared purposes.

The British artist Adrian Heath observed these features with the skilled eye of a painter:

I have always been fascinated by Mondrian's working methods, empirical procedures and execution. The craquelure that is evident in many of his canvases is an indication of his repeated adjustments to attain the exact shade of white, and his use of 'scotch tape', a temporary expedient in thickening a black line so that his eye could make judgement,

reveals an approach that owes nothing to calculation or pre-planning. It could even be said that Mondrian was an action painter working in slow motion. It is certain that he belonged to the category of artist who derives stimulus from the medium, and to whom the execution of the work is a pleasure as well as a necessity.

Heath is drawing attention to the emotional and intuitive aspects of Mondrian's procedures. Each painting presented the artist with an infinite

number of possible adjustments of the vertical and horizontal black lines, each generating a new configuration of the primary colour and white planes. Every painting in Mondrian's instantly recognisable mature style represents, then, another attempt at the realisation of an ideal beyond the contingencies of the ineluctable actual. Each painting reminds us of the impossibility of such a realisation. This is the tragic irony at the heart of Mondrian's beautiful project.

2

ABSTRACTION AND THE VISIBLE

CUBISM, PHOTOGRAPHY AND PERSPECTIVE

It has often been thought that photography released painting from the burden of representation, and thereby paved the way for abstraction. Painting could develop its own abstract forms, exploiting the properties specific to the medium itself: line and plane, colour and shape on the flat surface of the support. It could dissociate itself from the fictions and tricks of naturalism: shading, modelling and imitative colour; the creation of illusionistic space and lighting 'effects'; the description of objects and topographies; the delineation of face and figure; moral or dramatic narrative. It could seek pure self-definition, and in doing so create imageries that were analogues of the energies hidden behind the veil of natural appearances. These energies might be physical (manifest in light, forms and movement), mental (manifest in language, signs and symbols, in geometries and diagrams), moral or spiritual (manifest in feelings and ideas). Jan Tschichold, the great Dutch typographer, put this view succinctly in his 1935 classic, *Asymmetric Typography*:

The subject is not of great importance to a good painter – it merely provides him with the opportunity to paint significant relationships of colour and form … The painter is no longer the only person who can represent our world 'as we see it'. The photographer can do that better and more quickly and he can do it in colour too … Hence the representation of things can often be left to the photographer. Since the invention of photography the task of painting has been to explore colour and form on flat surface.

Tschichold, and the many others who attributed the new freedoms of abstraction to the redundancy of representation brought about by photography, were, in fact, quite wrong. Photography actually had its profoundest effects on painting 'with a subject'. It is truer to say that abstraction followed from a number of developments in figurative painting that together constituted a complex (and in certain respects, unconscious) challenge to those very claims for photography that it represented the visual world as we really experience it. The most significant of these developments was Cubism, which actively sought to picture objects and events in ways that were not possible for the camera. Picasso's deep fascination with photography (as both practitioner and collector) during the years of his Cubist researches reflects a critical preoccupation with the *differences* between the two media, precisely when he was most committed to the discovery of radical new ways to represent *how* we see the world.

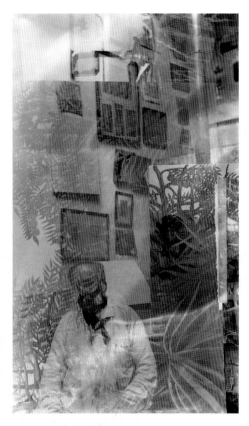

Picasso recognised that the viewpoint of the photograph is fixed, its visual field arbitrary, and that it fixes the specific time of the exposure of the plate to light. (His own photographic experiments with superimposition were efforts, perhaps, to get round these limitations or to demonstrate them explicitly; fig.17.) Photography does not represent to the viewer a personally expressive active intervention in the world, the making of a sign or a message, open to interpretation within complex codes. It is the outcome of a chemical reaction that registers gradations of light and tone. As Roland Barthes suggested, the photograph is 'a message without a code'. It is the caption, the linguistic accompaniment or the context that instates it within a coded discourse and gives it possibilities of meaning that go beyond the arbitrary. Of course, photographs are 'taken' (a revealing term) by somebody, and with purpose, but that does not alter the fact that what a photograph registers – the image of its subject – is a function of that chemical process; it is an index, or trace, of an aspect of temporal reality rather than a symbolic representation of it. A photograph does not present to the eye what a thing looks like: it merely registers what a thing 'looks like' *to the camera*. The camera does not 'look', it has no eye; it does not construct a visual reality on the basis of what is known and felt within a continuous consciousness and a dynamically developing knowledge. Those are functions of *being*, of human agency. It is merely mechanical. To adapt Walter Benjamin's

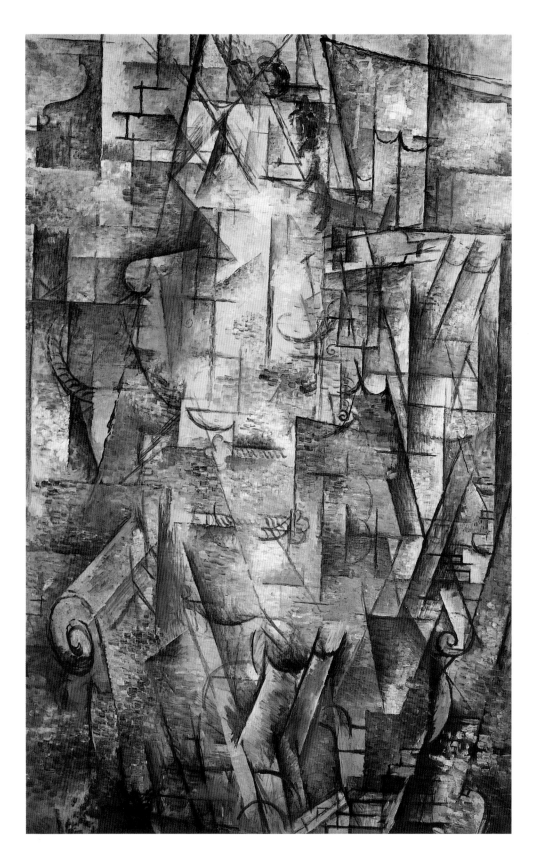

phrase, the camera is 'optically unconscious'; and aware of nothing, it can neither lie nor tell the truth.

Picasso and Braque, in the period of their close association, from 1908 to 1914, the years of Analytic and early Synthetic Cubism, were involved in a strenuously active interrogation of visual reality that had its immediate precedent in the work of Cézanne, whom they greatly admired. There is more to the processes of 'seeing' than the purely visual. Cézanne's greatness, and his enormous significance for modern painting, consisted in his courageous acknowledgement of the complexity of visual perception, and in his recognition of its implications for painting. 'There are two things in the painter, the eye and the mind: each of them should aid the other. It is necessary to work at their mutual development, in the eye by looking at nature, in the mind by the logic of organised sensations which provide the means of expression.' A 'logic of organised sensations' is a precise description of what the Cubism of Braque, Picasso, Léger and Juan Gris sought to achieve. In so doing (the seeking here is of more consequence than the achieving) they made painting once again 'a thing of the mind', by admitting to its process the operation of the constructive faculties of conception. (Leonardo described painting as *cosa mentale*: a definition of which Picasso was well aware.) Painting is 'not concerned with the reconstitution of an anecdotal fact', wrote Braque, 'but with the *constitution* of a pictorial fact'.

The Cubists, even as they moved decisively away from the imitation of appearances towards an emphasis on the painting as an autonomous work, as 'a pictorial fact' – a thing *composed* – never lost sight of visible nature. Indeed, their search was for new ways to represent the visible world, or rather, to reinvent it through painting in such a way as to be true to the nature of seeing itself. 'Seeing' is not *believing*: belief in what one sees, recognising it as true to reality, involves complicated mental operations, aspects of *knowing*, aspects of doubt, a kind of questioning. 'What forces our interest is Cézanne's anxiety – that's Cézanne's lesson,' said Picasso many years later. The French critic Maurice Merleau-Ponty wrote movingly of Cézanne's enduring doubt about the success of his life-long effort to be true to his perception of the world, quoting a revealing exchange with the younger artist Emile Bernard: 'But are not nature and art different?' – 'I would like to make them one. Art is a personal perception. This perception I place in feeling and I ask of intelligence that it should organise it into a work.' To see the world truly is to compose it, to bring our thought and feeling to our sensations, to *re*-present it to the mind as something comprehensible. 'The senses deform, the mind forms', wrote Braque, for whom the sense of sight was as intense as only a great artist's can be.

Let us look at Braque's *Woman Reading* 1911 (fig.18) in the light of these considerations. The almost life-size figure in the painting is little more than a ghost, more of a radiant absence than a presence. She appears to be seated in an armchair, the scroll-ended arms of which are visible lower left and lower right. One of the wings of the chair-back, its position registering a slight recession appropriate to its position in space, at upper-centre left, half-rhymes with the chair-arm below it. The position of the woman's face, at top centre, is indicated by smudges that appear to describe her dark hair. We can identify some short lengths of what appears to be furniture cord or rope at centre and centre left, and an architectural bracket (of a mantelpiece, or a decorative feature of a cupboard?) at top left. Where the woman's bust might be is a passage of pure light. In fact, the 'woman' of the title is dissolved into the painting, which has gone its own way towards an arrangement of strokes, stipples, lines and planes. These are vertically composed around an abstract linear structure, a trapezium described by the two more or less continuous divergent lines from top centre, which are met at matching angles by two diagonal movements from the lower edge. In spite of the name given to the style, this picturing is anything but 'analytic' in the scientific or critical senses of the term. Rather, we might describe its organisation as analogous to that of contrapuntal music: it is a composition of passages of tones and half-tones, of subtle harmonies of whites, greys, ochres and browns, its countless short dashes and tiny strokes like notes held in restless tension by an order of lines, curves and arabesques.

What can be the meaning of this 'visual music'? What has happened to the ostensible subject? We might recall Mondrian's desired 'destruction of melody': the elimination of description and negation of emotion. Braque's composing devices are, however, very different from Mondrian's orthogonal 'equilibrium'; their effects are more lyrical, more poignant. 'Lyrical' is Braque's own word for what is happening in the painting. Let me elaborate, with parentheses, one of his 'Reflections on Art', 1917: 'The subject [of the painting] is not the object [in this case, the woman reading], it is a new unity [this is the new 'subject' of the painting], a lyricism which grows completely from the means [the medium and its manipulation].' This is to say that it is the act of painting that creates the poetic truth; it is the artist who *constructs* the image. This making of the picture is something similar to the complex of perception and conception that constitutes our true experience of 'seeing'. *Woman Reading* is as much a painting about the act of painting its subject, that is, about the nature of *seeing* the natural object, as it is a painting *of* the subject. What is presented to the eye are fragments, suggestions, adumbrations, with some fairly perfunctory indications of the recognisable facts. What is asserted, in purely *pictorial* terms, is that we encounter the world visually as a succession of moments, nanoseconds of perception, organising it continuously (and mostly unconsciously) into a coherence that is necessarily personal to the perceiver. Its dizzying structure of fragments demonstrates to the viewer the other great fact of perception: that the eye shifts constantly from object to object, aspect to aspect, stimulating the brain to *construct* rather than reconstruct what it 'sees' into a coherent *mental* image. The painting imitates how we actually create the world with eye and mind.

Braque spoke of the process of fragmentation as a means by which he could get as close to the objects of the world as painting might permit. It brought them into what he called 'tactile space', a pictorial space that resembled the actual space in which we live and within which, when we see things, we have a sense of their textures and of their vital relation to our own body. This is not, however, the space of perspective, where imaginary lines converge to a vanishing point, things are given body by modulated tonalities and the

19
Pablo Picasso

The Mandolin Player
1911

Oil on canvas
100.5 × 69.5
(39½ × 27⅜)
Fondation Beyeler,
Basel

diminishing scale creates the illusion that things are receding into the distance. For the Cubists traditional perspective was subject to the same limitations as the space of photography. '[It] gave me no satisfaction', said Braque. 'It is too mechanical to allow one to take full possession of things. It has its origins in the single viewpoint and never gets away from it. But the viewpoint is of little importance.' That 'possession of things' is 'the coherence which is necessarily

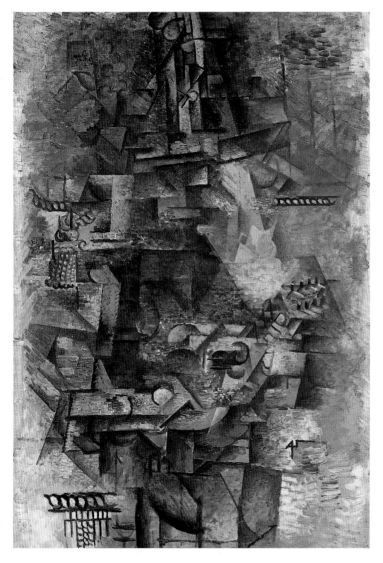

personal to the perceiver'. It is the coherence of *sight*, coming not simply from what is seen by the eye but what is known by the mind. And the mind knows more about the objects that the hand depicts than what is immediately visible to the eye. For Braque the crucial aspect of this reality was spatial, and a painting such as *Woman Reading* asks us to imagine the strokes, stipples, lines and facets of paint out of which it is created as the flicker, beam and darkness of light and shadow, playing in time across the subject. Space is defined by light. The painting's almost monochromatic unity of tone is a device to create harmony – a metaphor for coherence. A beautiful harmonic chord is held as an equivalence for the painting's true subject: the shimmering light of a moment in a room; not so much a representation of things as a presentation of time in space.

Picasso's *Mandolin Player* 1911 (fig.19) has aspects of pictorial structure in common with *Woman Reading*: most notably the divergent/convergent trapezium that is the principal vertical dynamic. But the painting is darker, more problematic. Where the Braque seems centrifugal – scattering outwards the facets and flickers of light – this seems centripetal, as if coherence is not to be found in the harmony of light in space so much as in a powerful impulse to form. If the Braque is about the dissolve of the complex manifold into a harmonious insubstantiality, the Picasso is about the willing of undifferentiated matter into substantial form. In this case the fixed viewpoint and frozen time of photography and perspective are contradicted by the energy that is bringing into being, *and into sight*, the neck of the instrument (its tuning pegs at a steep angle) and the hand of the player that is grasping it. The decisive painting of the great tassel (a bell-pull, a plush curtain tie-back?) and of the furniture braiding at lower left and upper right also serve to convey the powerful impression of things being brought into being, and into perceptibility. Even as you look, these things seem to cohere into solidity out of a dark penumbra. Other forms, less 'readable', nevertheless seem more block-like, more substantial than Braque's *passages* of light.

For our purposes the similarities between the Analytic Cubism of Braque and of Picasso are more important than the differences, though the differences are interesting and prefigure in many ways developments in abstraction. It is as if their paintings at this time, so similar in many ways, were the outcome of almost opposite impulses: Braque's to the re-invention of light and space as the precondition of presenting the momentarily poised reality of the object; Picasso's to the magical transformation of matter into form, effected by the will of the artist, and proposing metamorphosis as a condition of reality. But what do they have in common, and why is it so important to the history of abstract art?

To begin with, it is that they so decisively abolished the central importance of the *subject* to painting. Ideas and meanings in painting had always followed from the subject (religious or historical, portrait, landscape or still life) and from the mode of its *re*-presentation, whether in terms of perspectival space as a narrative or dramatic *mise-en-scène*, for example, or of Impressionist realisations of objects and events in the natural light and colour of the perceived world. But from this time on, it was possible to think of ideas as finding expression in the act and medium of painting itself, of painting *as* thinking, or as a material metaphor for the processes by which the eye and the mind apprehend the world and turn it into meaning. (This is not to suggest that Picasso and Braque did not care about their subjects or did not choose them with deliberation. That they were mostly familiar, recognisable objects or real people was useful to their purposes.) Cézanne, in recognising that his *sensations* — the complex dynamics of his perception/conception of what he called 'the motif' — were actually his true subject, was the great trail-blazer in this quest for truth to reality. In his mature work he developed a painterly means that could express this dialectic of sensation, of seeing/knowing. This was the technique of '*passages*', by which he meant transitions of thin, flat strokes (the direct precursors of the Cubist facet or plane), parallel to the picture plane and clearly visible as pigmented medium. These created a kind of abstract contrapuntal music on the flat surface even as they described receding, pictorial space. The 'picture' was, so to speak, simultaneously a 'painting'.

The second major change brought about by Cubism, and this follows directly from the first, was in the relation of the viewer to the work. The painting was no longer to be regarded as a pictorial representation of objects and events fixed in illusionistic space, replete with specific references and encoded in accord with particular religious, moral or historical ideas or conventions. It was, rather, to be apprehended as an object in the world, actively demanding the construction of possible meanings by the spectator. The goal of a painting was the '*constitution* of a pictorial fact'. The meanings of this object (this 'pictorial fact') were not fixed, and could not be, for they were in every case the outcome of the unique encounter of the viewer and the object. A kind of Copernican revolution had been effected. Whereas, before, the subject of the painting was crucial to its meaning, now it was the viewer who had become, in a manner of speaking, the expressive subject, the creator of its meanings. In the process of *looking* these remain unspoken and, to all intents and purposes, beyond verbal expression. For many artists, including Malevich and Mondrian, it followed that the work no longer had to 'represent' any object at all: it presented itself *as* an object, and it was the viewer who gave it meaning. 'With time it became clear to me', wrote Mondrian in 1936, 'that Cubism did not accept the logical consequences of its own discoveries; it was not taking abstraction to its ultimate goal ... the goal of expressing pure reality. I felt that true contemplation of [the higher] reality could only be achieved by purely pictorial means.' 'Purely pictorial' here means purely *abstract*. In their own later work the great Cubists refuted this logic: they remained passionately committed to art as a refraction of the natural reality of the visible world.

PURE PAINTING AND THE NEW 'REALISM'

Fernand Léger quickly understood that although the Cubist approach had freed painting from the requirement to imitate nature, it still engaged with material actualities. His imagination was keyed to the noise and dynamism of modern life, excited by the machine, energised by the idea of speed. Like Picasso and Braque, whose work he saw and admired from 1910 onwards, he had looked with intelligent intensity at Cézanne and seen clearly that the master had come to the very boundary of representation but had never crossed it: 'what he made came completely from his own genius, and if he had had creative imagination, he would have spared himself from "going to the motif" or setting up still life arrangements in front of himself.' With *Woman in Blue* 1912 (fig.20), Léger considered that he had liberated himself from Cézanne and 'the melody of impressionism'. The constructive scheme of the picture is, characteristically, spiral. The splintered light of Braque and the emergent forms of Picasso give way here to a free-wheeling regatta of sail-like shapes in pure colours. The pictorial clues – the glass with spoon on the corner of a table, the turned chair-leg, the colour of the woman's dress – are unambiguous, but they are assimilated into a composition of abstract contrasts: of colours (blues/whites/blacks/reds, etc.); tones (light/dark, ochres/greys); and forms (curved/angular). *Woman in Blue* is intended to dominate its space and draw the eye irresistibly into a dance of forms that has transformed its ostensible subject into a dynamic of mental sensations. In 1913 Léger went on to make a number of paintings – the nearest Cubism ever came to pure abstraction – in which the subject is altogether replaced by the pure play of colour and shape contrasts. Even in the most extreme of these, such as *Contrast of Forms* (fig.21), their quasi-geometry is that of things *as seen* in the world: they twist and spin like metal machine parts, or saucepans or buckets, seeming to catch the light of day with a sharp, percussive visual clarity.

Speaking in early 1913, with these paintings clearly in mind, Léger re-defined 'realism' in terms of the disposition of formal elements in a painting rather than as a style of representation. (Both Malevich and Mondrian were to follow him in this usage but, as we have seen, with quite different purposes in mind.) Léger meant that the exciting reality of modern life – its speed, its fragmentation, its sudden ruptures, its contrasts, its simultaneous and multiple sensory impressions – should find expression in the relations of abstract forms on the canvas. These could be conceived of as active analogues for the energy and movement of the *objective* world: 'the *realistic* value of a work is completely independent of any imitative character … pictorial realism is the simultaneous ordering of three great plastic components: Lines, Forms, and Colours.' Given the popular developments of photography and film, fiction and theatre, plastic art could, he wrote, 'logically limit itself to its own purpose: *realism of conception*'. The 'logic' of this was clear: '*Each art is isolating itself and limiting itself to its own domain*. It is logical, for by limiting itself to its own purposes, it enables achievements to be intensified.' The domain of painting was that 'simultaneous ordering' of formal elements distinctive to it, for the 'realism of conception' entailed the elimination of 'visual, sentimental, representational, and popular

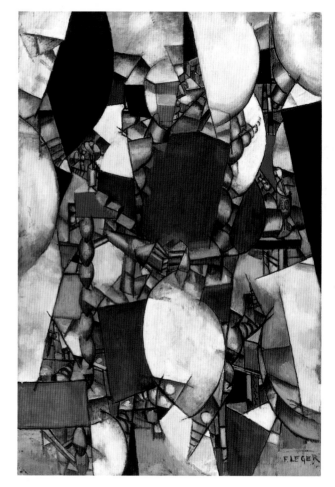

subject matter'. This is a remarkable formulation, anticipating what was to become, in the 1960s and after, a dogmatic reductive definition of what constitutes 'modernist painting'. After the war Léger quickly found his own way back to a style of decorative representation with a subject matter that reflected a grave and beautiful socialist vision, a belief in the democratic basis of modern life. But he had, in his earlier writings and in his own version of Cubism, clarified the idea of the painting-as-object, as a thing in itself, a kind of machine for visualising the energies in material things.

It is sometimes suggested that Cubism, in its recourse to visual relativity and complex time, had in some way a scientific basis; that its discoveries were parallel to those of contemporary physicists and mathematicians, or experimental psychologists. And it is indeed true that there was much talk during those years in the studios and cafés of Paris about the new relativist advances in the sciences. But art is poetic and philosophical, it is not scientific. The nature of the intuition and experiment by which it proceeds is different in kind from that of science, and its success is determined not by objective tests but by its reception within the critical discourse and its impact upon its various publics. Even so, the findings of science had an enormous impact upon the imagination of artists, who turned them to creative use. And the idea of science, as a process of research and discovery, was often used as a metaphor by those who wrote about modern art, especially abstraction. This was inevitable, since science rather than religion had come to be seen in the new century as the means to the establishment of reality and natural truth, and was therefore a model for any activity that sought to engage with those great intangibles, and be true to the real.

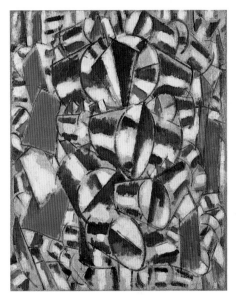

Guillaume Apollinaire, the poet-critic friend of avant-garde artists in Paris during the heroic years of experiment before the First World War, was the most perceptive commentator on their activities, and a tireless publicist for them. 'The young painters of the avant-garde schools', he wrote in an article in early 1912, 'wish to do pure painting. Theirs is an entirely new plastic art. It is only at its beginnings and is not yet as abstract as it would like to be. The new painters are in a sense mathematicians without knowing it, but they have not yet abandoned nature, and they examine it carefully.' Mathematics is of course the purest science, dealing as it does with the purely abstract, whether numbers or geometric forms. How did Apollinaire define 'pure painting'? It was painting that had no 'real subject', for which imitation had no importance, in which 'the artist sacrifices everything to the composition of his picture' and that required the viewer 'to find in [it] a different kind of pleasure from that which he can as easily find in the spectacle of nature'. This new art would be to the old kind of painting 'what music is to literature'. Music is the most abstract of the arts, an art of pure (aural) forms and relations; pure painting would provide 'artistic sensations' derived exclusively from the 'harmony of lights and shades and independent of the subject depicted'. Cubism was 'the art of painting new configurations with elements drawn not from visual but from conceptual reality'. Its geometric aspect was an outcome of its 'rendering of an essential reality with great purity' from which 'the accidental or anecdotal aspects of the subject had been eliminated'. This elucidation of the idea of pure painting owed as much to Apollinaire's conversation with artist friends as to his own critical acumen and poetic inventiveness. It provides marvellous insights into the development of the polemical and critical language that justified and promoted the idea of a non-metaphysical abstract art at the historical moment of its inception. It was an abstraction not seeking transcendence but steadfastly rooted in the material world, its forms derived from the actualities of the visual, its ground the here and now of modern reality – hence its claims to be

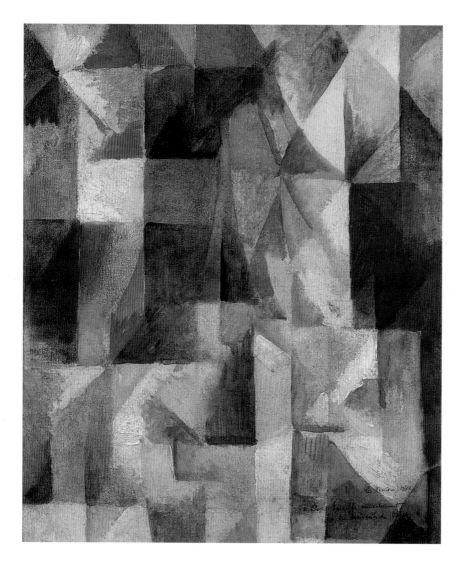

22
Robert Delaunay

Windows Open Simultaneously (First Part, Third Motif) 1912

Oil on canvas
45.7 × 37.5
(18¾ × 14¾)
Tate

23
Sonya Delaunay

Electric Prisms 1914

Oil on canvas
238 × 250 (93¾ × 98¾)
Musée D'Art Moderne, Paris

'the new realism': it was a development *from* representation, having purified it of referential redundancy.

Léger was not alone in developing the tendency in Cubism towards 'pure painting'. Husband and wife Robert and Sonia Delaunay, working closely together, had by 1913 arrived at a luminous abstraction, based not upon 'contrast of forms' but on what Robert described in manifesto statements in late 1912 (one of them published by Apollinaire) as the 'simultaneous contrasts' of *colours*. Delaunay used Cubist techniques of pictorial fracture, of dispositions of plane and facet, to paint again and again the view from a window over Paris, so it was not surprising that he should have become enraptured by light as the source of all visual reality. There are eleven other versions of *Windows Open* 1912 (fig.22), the 'motif' of which was actually taken from a postcard, indicating significantly that these were essentially imaginative works in which the creative focus was as much on the painting itself as on the static view of the city. Pure painting might be constructed not by Léger's 'lines and forms and colours' but by colours alone, which by their 'uneven quantities' can represent on the canvas the reality of light, without which there is no seeing, and no art. The artist seeks a sublime 'clarity' that is the expression on the canvas of a 'harmonic vision': 'the *synchronous movement* (simultaneity) *of light*

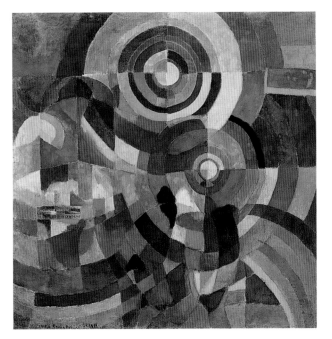

which is the *only reality*' becomes the true subject of painting.

What the work of the Delaunays had in common with that of their friend Léger in this crucial period just before the outbreak of the war was its marvellous dynamism, its vivid presentation of visually energetic contrasts and of the sensation of movement. It was the highly sensitive response of artists philosophically and psychologically attuned to the extraordinary changes in city life, to the arrival on the streets of the motor car, to developments in film and sound recording, above all to the emergence of a new spirit of technological modernism. Sonia's *Electric Prisms* 1914 (fig.23) perfectly exemplifies these qualities of response, its square format dynamically containing spinning, multi-coloured discs in simultaneous motion, controlled as within the closed system of a machine, with no possibility of sideways or vertical movement. Its colours, in complex chromatic contrasts, are laid on thinly to create the effect of transparency, as if brilliant light were entering through a radiant window. Here is an abstraction, like Léger's, that has its basis in the excitements of sensory experience, that seeks to enhance and heighten our experience of the actual visible. 'The subject of painting', wrote Robert, 'is exclusively plastic, and it results from [natural] vision. It must be the pure expression of human nature.' For the Delaunays the new age demanded a new, *abstract* realism.

3

ABSTRACTION IN THE WORLD: CONSTRUCTIVISMS

TATLIN'S DREAM

Nothing could have been in greater contrast to Malevich's Suprematist manifesto for the *0.10* exhibition in 1915 (see p.15), with its impassioned and self-mythologising rhetoric, than the modest pamphlet prepared for the same occasion by Vladimir Tatlin. This contained photographs of a number of his 'counter-reliefs' and a short text, ironic in its extreme matter-of-factness, which listed the group exhibitions to which he had submitted easel paintings, and noted that he had never belonged to any tendency (including 'Tatlinism'). It mentioned his first exhibition, at his own studio the previous year, in which he had first shown 'painterly reliefs', and listed the mundane materials he had used in their making: 'wood, metal, putty, glass, plaster, cardboard, gesso, tar, etc.; the surfaces of those materials were treated with putty, ripolin, sprinkled dust and other means.' It concluded: 'In 1915 Tatlin's studio produced "Corner Counter Reliefs", which are exhibited ... at *The Last Futurist Exhibition* in Petrograd'. The contrast between the publications reflected profound differences, both temperamental and ideological, between the two artists: Malevich, magisterial, charismatic, deeply mystical in spirit and of a metaphysical cast of mind; Tatlin, collaborative, pragmatic and experimental, philosophically materialist, committed to the idea of revolutionary change. Mutually antagonistic, they represent two distinct but at times closely interrelated tendencies in abstract art, and in the ideas that supported it. Tatlin, we may say, was the progenitor of the Constructivist idea in art. This was to become, in its various manifestations, the conceptual determinant of a modernist trend in art, architecture and design that developed into a major international movement touching virtually every aspect of modern life.

In Paris in early 1914 Tatlin had visited Picasso and Braque and had been greatly excited by their invention of collage and sculpture, which incorporated fragments of the real world (newspaper, grained wallpaper, spoons, bits of painted wood, etc.), and by the roughly made cardboard, wooden and metal wall reliefs, such as the sheet-metal *Guitar* 1912–13 (fig.24), in Picasso's studio. He would also have seen recent pictures in which Picasso had used everyday materials such as 'Ripolin' house paint, and mixed sand and gesso with oil paint. The constructions, the first such sculptures ever made, provided Tatlin with the clue he needed to make his own, even more radical, breakaway from traditional ('easel') painting, and led directly to his invention, in mid-1914, of the completely abstract 'counter-relief'. This led in its turn to the revolutionary 'corner counter-reliefs' of 1915, shown at *0.10*. Almost everything Tatlin made during this period was lost, presumed destroyed, in Stalinist times. There are some rare survivals: *Painterly Relief* 1914–17 (fig.25) found its way into the Costakis collection in c.1960. Although completely abstract. it shows Tatlin still working within an aesthetic that owes something to Cubist collages such as Braque's *Guitar* 1913 (fig.26), with its overlay of planes, its counterpoint of curved and straight lines, and its diagonal dynamic. But in this, and in the tempera-on-wood paintings he made some time after it, such as *Untitled* 1916–17 (fig.27), Tatlin had made a creative quantum leap: from the picture to the iconic object, in which the materials are as significant as the image.

24
Pablo Picasso

Guitar 1912–13
(winter)

Construction of sheet metal and wire
77.5 × 35 × 19.3
(30½ × 13¾ × 7⅝)
The Museum of Modern Art, New York. Gift of the artist

In Paris Picasso continued to make playful constructions, such as the witty *Violin* of late 1915 (fig.28), in which the instrument's swell and arabesque are perversely translated into plane and straight line, its polished wood into painted sheet metal. It confounds our response to the title: confronted by the object we are asked to re-imagine the subject of the work. Tatlin's *Corner Counter Relief* 1915 (fig.29), constructed quite probably within weeks of *Violin*, has, however, no subject of that kind at all. It marks a new beginning as radical in its implications for sculpture as those of the *Black Suprematist Square* (fig.1) for painting, and more far-reaching in its effects. Now we can only imaginatively appreciate its impact through photographs or by means of a number of reconstructions made by the sculptor Martyn Chalk in 1979–82. Its formal innovation consisted in its realisation of actual relations between material and space, positive and negative, light and shadow: relations different in kind from those of Picasso's contemporary constructions, whose 'representational' volumetrics still operate within the fictional logic of the 'pictorial'. Occupying the real space of the spectator, unlimited by any frame, its interactions are those of the energetic world, governed by gravity and tension. At *0.10* the *Corner Counter Relief* was stretched across the corner of the room, placed, like Malevich's *Black Suprematist Square* in the same exhibition (see fig.2), in the traditional position of the family icon. Both were thus provocatively presented as new icons, but with quite different intentions. For whereas Malevich was appropriating the function of the family icon, providing a new focus for *spiritual* contemplation, Tatlin was replacing the mystical object altogether with an objective demonstration of the 'movement, tension and interrelationships' of the *material* world. In a manifesto

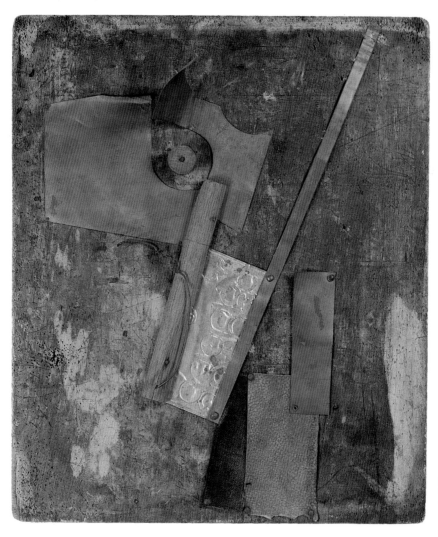

25
Vladimir Yevgrafovich Tatlin

Painterly Relief
1914–17

Wood, metal and iron
63 × 53 (24¾ × 20⅞)
Tretyakov Gallery, Moscow

26
Georges Braque

Guitar 1913 (summer)

Gesso, pasted papers, charcoal, pencil and gouache on canvas
99.7 × 65.1
(39¼ × 25⅝)
The Museum of Modern Art, New York. Acquired through the Willie B. Bliss Bequest

27
Vladimir Yevgrafovich Tatlin

Untitled 1916–17

Tempera on wood
75.5 × 41.5
(29¾ × 16⅜)
Private Collection.
Courtesy Annely Juda Fine Art, London

28
Pablo Picasso

Violin 1915

Mixed media
100 × 63 × 18
(39⅜ × 24¾ × 7⅛)
Musée Picasso, Paris

29
Vladimir Yevgrafovich Tatlin

Corner Counter Relief
(reconstruction by Martyn Chalk)

1915 (reconstructed 1979–82)

Mixed media
78.8 × 152.4 × 76.2
(31 × 60 × 30)
Annely Juda Fine Art, London

of 1921 Tatlin went so far as to claim that these works of 1914–15 actually anticipated the Revolution of 1917, establishing by prophetic analogy the creative 'principle' of 'material, volume and construction'. 'Construction' is to be defined here as the active process by which humankind creates the world and its objects. Tatlin claimed for his works a creative purpose in this process.

Nicolei Puni, an early critical champion of Tatlin, characterised these works as explicitly 'against Cubism'. The Cubist destruction of 'banal' perspective and

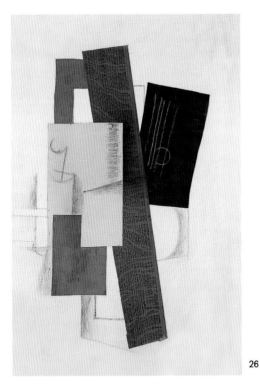

26

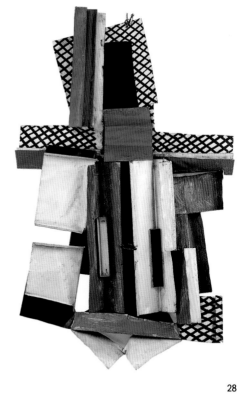

28

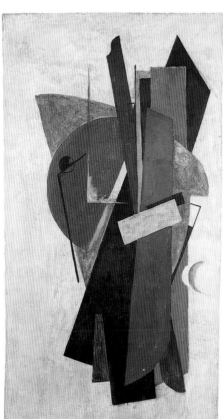

27

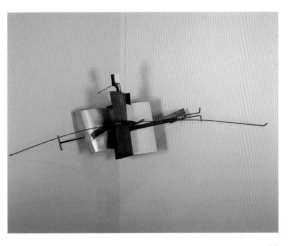

29

its attempt to introduce 'the sequence of time' had been heroic but in vain. 'One had to look for the way out not merely beyond the canvas but beyond the whole ['subject'-based] tradition of European art. This way out has been found by those artists strong enough to study dimensions in real spatial relationships.' The materials and their relations in Tatlin's reliefs were presented as what they were, not as a means to the representation of anything else. Unlike all art since the Renaissance, his constructions did not picture an aspect of the world. They did not reflect reality; they were components of reality, a part of the world, with their own visible and exemplary dynamics. In this, they were categorically

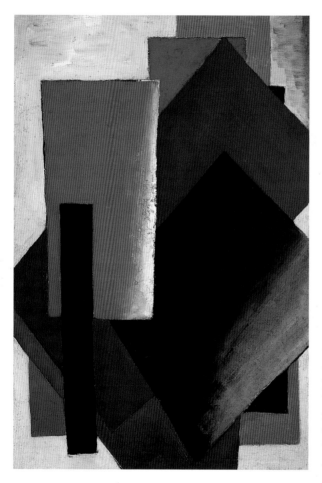

different even from 'pure painting', which was still confined to the canvas and treated 'subjects' – light, energy, speed, movement – that were external to itself. In his 1921 manifesto 'The Work Ahead of Us' Tatlin reiterated his slogans of 1913: 'Let us place the eye under the control of touch' and 'Through the discovery of material to [the creation of] a new object'. The logic of this was that art should play a role in the world at large, acting not only as a model of human creativity but as an agency for political and social construction. Tatlin, like Malevich (whose politics and 'economics' were essentially metaphysical), identified with the 1917 Revolution; both were active, as theorists, teachers and administrators, in the new

30
Liubov Popova
Painterly Architectonic
1916
Oil on board
59.4 × 39.4
(23⅜ × 15½)
Scottish National
Gallery of Modern Art,
Edinburgh

31
Alexander Rodchenko
White Circle 1918
Oil on canvas
89.2 × 71.5
(35⅛ × 28⅛)
Russian State Museum,
Leningrad

32
Alexander Rodchenko
Black on Black 1918
Oil on canvas
84 × 66.5 (33⅛ × 26⅛)
Russian State Museum,
Leningrad

institutions of art education. The world seemed to be 'turned upside down', abstract painting and collage were promulgated as actively expressive of ideas that in the political-social sphere would change the world.

Under Malevich's powerful influence, many progressive artists committed themselves at first to Suprematism as a sufficiently revolutionary redefinition of art. Like Tatlin, whose studio she shared in late 1914, Liubov Popova had also spent time in Paris and was aware of *papier collé*, collage and constructed reliefs as developments of late Analytic Cubism. At *0.10* she exhibited a number of figurative painted cardboard reliefs in a Cubist-derived style. Then, inspired by

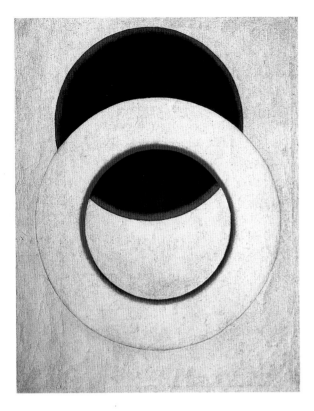

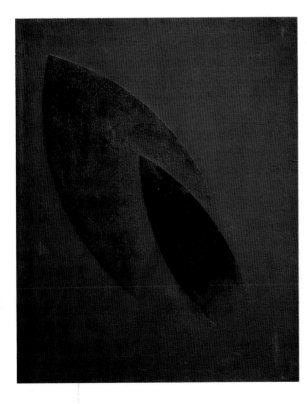

Malevich, she began to paint completely abstract 'Suprematist' compositions. But the title *Painterly Architectonic* 1916 (fig.30) (which she gave to many of her paintings) suggests that, even as a Suprematist, Popova was more interested in painting as a projection of material reality than as the personal expression of a metaphysical vision. The programme behind these paintings has, in fact, much in common with Tatlin's: the abstract plane of the collage fragment, whose material actuality emphasises the objective surface of the support, is liberated from the fictional world of the Cubist image. Where Malevich's Suprematism visualises dynamic relations in metaphysical space, Popova's superimposed planes of strong colour have the objective presence of 'paint as such'. Pressing up to the surface, *they are what they are*, just as the tempera and the wood of Tatlin's paintings, and the iron, aluminium and zinc components of his *Counter Reliefs* are actual materials, presented 'as such' and not as 'media' for the representation of 'a subject'. The reality of the painting, like that of the construction, is that of a thing assembled, its components held together by 'architectonic' principles. It is at once a visible model of creative energy, and the objective evidence or trace of such energy in constructive action.

In the early years of the Bolshevik Revolution Popova and other artists quickly moved towards the practical deployment of their constructive energies in broader cultural, social and educational activities. Alexander Rodchenko and his wife Varvara Stepanova, inspired by Tatlin, had by late 1919 committed themselves to a utilitarian art at the service of the Revolution. In Rodchenko's paintings images of precise geometric forms —

lines, circles, rectangles – as opposed to Malevich's approximate geometric signs, are conceived as demonstrative of actual spatial relations, and of the behaviour of light and colour in objective space. They are manifestly constructed out of real materials; their geometry is impersonal, inexpressive, universal. *White Circle* (fig.31) and *Black on Black* (fig.32), both 1918, are deliberate responses to Suprematist painting with its other-worldly pretensions, specifically, to Malevich's ethereal *White on White* paintings of 1917 and 1918. Both Rodchenko's paintings create illusions of space. In the former a halo of dark blue gives the black disc a shimmer as of an object in cosmic space, while the inner edge of the white circle, red and in part blue, serves visually to separate it as an object floating, in perfectly symmetrical relation, in front of the disc. In *Black on Black* the differentiations of black are achieved by mixing 'non-art' materials with the oil paint and applying lacquer to the surface to create variations that respond to the circumambient light. In *Suprematism* 1918 (fig.33) the image strives towards its own dissolution, towards invisibility; *Black on Black* insists on the visibility of space and the tactility of matter. Its rising forms, appearing to emerge out of chaos, are at once manifest stuff and emblematic images of the constructive energies of the material world.

For Rodchenko easel painting would be taken to the limit of its material self-definition, whereafter it would be superseded by the deployment of constructive energies in the actual world. In 1921, at the Moscow exhibition $5 \times 5 = 25$, he showed the ultimate formal paintings, three entirely monochrome canvases (red, blue and yellow), thus freeing colour from any kind of purely artistic task, insisting on it as a constructive principle, an objective quality of things in the world. With this, Rodchenko ceased painting, and moved into photography and design, working closely with Stepanova, who also renounced individualistic aesthetic endeavour in favour of 'useful' work. At the First State Textile Works she and Popova revolutionised textile design by limiting it to a strictly geometric repertoire of circles, stripes, rectangles and triangles, abstract patterns with no 'expressive' or descriptive function, appropriate to the mechanical manufacture of materials for the people of an egalitarian socialist society. Popova eloquently stated the 'productivist' position:

Even the new objective method of analysing the formal elements of each individual 'art' … is still, ultimately, concerned with the same old depictive formal elements … [We must] find the paths and methods that lead away from the dead impasse of depictive art and advance through knowledge of technological production to a method of creating objects of industrial production, products of organised, material design.

This, then, was Tatlin's dream: of art as the imaginative projection, in concrete analogies, of the new possibilities of civilised life, and a constructive methodology for their material achievement in the forms of everyday life. Art was conceived as actively philosophical, effectively political and technologically productive.

DE STIJL, PROUN, MERZ: INTERNATIONAL CONSTRUCTIVISM

The dream of art as the aesthetic construction of the entire urban environment was not confined to the Russian avant garde. We have encountered it already in

33
Kazimir Malevich

Suprematism (White on White) 1918

Oil on canvas
97 × 70 (38¼ × 27½)
Stedelijk Museum, Amsterdam

the utopian idealism of Mondrian: 'we will be able to do without abstract-real "painting" as soon as we are able to transfer its beauty to our surroundings, through the disposition of colour in our interiors.' Mondrian remained committed to easel painting as an essentially philosophical activity concerned with realising ideal relations in 'plastic' terms. He was nevertheless for some years closely associated with the magazine *De Stijl*, founded in 1917 by the artist and theorist Theo van Doesburg in neutral Holland during the darkest days of

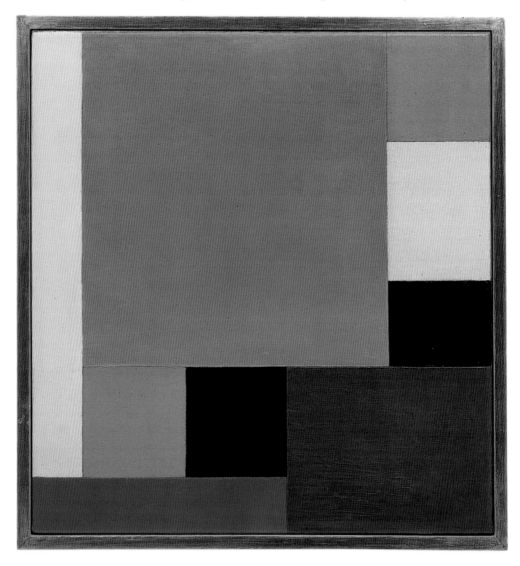

the war. *De Stijl* was founded to promote visual art as the means of defining the formal relations that could be utilised in design and architecture. Painting could demonstrate the universal principles of harmony that would govern human consciousness in the new world. These principles would then determine the new forms of modern architecture and design. Each of these creative activities had responsibility for the definition of the forms appropriate to itself, the better to play its distinctive part in the creation of the perfect environment.

Art, architecture and design would come together in an environmental harmony based on aesthetic principles that had been properly defined by each activity in its own terms.

Mondrian regarded his own mature style as the quintessential expression of this ideal general aesthetic, and he belongs in that visionary company of early abstractionists for whom the purpose of painting was the symbolic projection of a utopian future: 'abstract-real painting is only a *preparation* for the reshaping of our society and our environment.' Neo-Plastic painting, effecting a transformation of the mind and spirit, would make way for the realisation of the new city based on its principles: 'At present, Neo-Plasticism manifests in painting what will one day surround us in the form of sculpture and architecture.' There were practical professional men, like Jan Tschichold, who saw this already happening: ' the new typography does not derive from the new architecture', he wrote in 1935; 'rather both derive from the new painting, which has given to both a new significance of form. The new painting, by which we mean non-representative or abstract painting, originated before the new architecture and the latter could not have been conceived without the former'. This both exaggerates and over-simplifies. Adolf Loos's famous polemic 'Ornament and Crime' had appeared in 1908, and his pre-war architecture (and that of others) anticipated many of the features of the international modern style. Even so, the new abstract painting was conceived as sharing a profound social purpose with the utilitarian arts of architecture, design and typography. In considering international Constructivists as diverse as van Doesburg, El Lizzitsky, Naum Gabo and László Moholy-Nagy, we should be aware of the idealistic humanism that imbued their work with such potency of meaning for its creators and their public.

De Stijl certainly influenced the development of modernist architecture and design. Generally orthogonal, rectangular, with clean, straight lines and clear planes of primary colour, and black and white, it repudiates ornament and insists on the unity of materials and forms. Van Doesburg's painting *Composition XXII* 1920 (fig.34) exemplifies this, though in certain of his earlier paintings he had used pinks, greens, purples as well as the primaries, and two years later he was to adopt diagonal compositions that disrupted not only the static equilibrium of orthogonal painting but also ended his professional friendship with his mentor Mondrian, who could not countenance a deviation from the orthogonal absolute. *Composition XXII*, unlike Mondrian's post-1921 paintings, is created entirely out of juxtaposed planes. There are no black dividing lines theoretically capable of movement left or right, or up and down: the effect is of an absolute finality, each plane abutted to the next like different-sized building blocks held firmly in place by gravity and by the framing edges. The flatness of these planes is utterly objective; they are nothing more or less than rectangular areas of colour on the surface. For van Doesburg this monumental architectonics of colour represented a specifically Dutch 'neo-Cubist' victory over the 'remnants of the Picasso-Braque school'. He admired the young artists of the so-called Section d'Or he had recently seen in Paris, 'who present us', he wrote, 'with pure colour and *anti-modelé* [anti-tonal modelling] ... in other words, the battle for colour'. He had also been impressed by Léger's ideas of a 'polychrome architecture' and by the work of the painter-architect Charles-Eduoard Jeanneret, or Le Corbusier, as he was to become known.

By the mid-1920s van Doesburg had repudiated the strict observance of the 'Neo-Plastic' horizontal/vertical axis as a ruling principal for art and architecture. In close contact with the brilliant Russian painter, typographer and architectural theorist El Lizzitsky, and with other European Constructivists, he was directly engaged in architectural projects. Indeed, he had come in 1924 to a conclusion similar to that of the Russian productivists: that 'the true place of colour [was] in architecture ... that painting without architectural construction (that is easel painting) has no further reason for

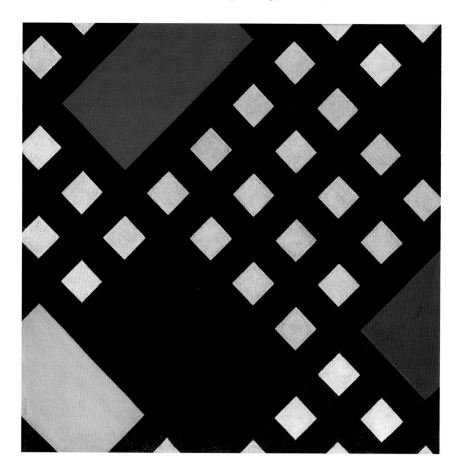

existence'. In spite of this, he continued to paint. *Counter Composition XV* (fig.35) of 1925 may be seen as a kind of objective manifesto for a new modernist aesthetic, 'elementarism', which countered static orthogonal dualism (horizontal = physical/vertical = spiritual) with the dynamic of the diagonal (= movement/energy). This spirited modernism informed his designs for the café-cinema in the night-club Café Aubette in Strasbourg in 1926, which employed dramatic 'elementarist' diagonals as a two-dimensional spatial counter-movement to the three-dimensional orthogonal architecture (fig.36). The designs were never popular, and the interiors were destroyed in 1928, but they remain symbolic of an important aspect of the *de Stijl* project.

Van Doesburg's environments, and the philosophy behind them, were deeply influenced by his contacts with El Lizzitsky, whose *Prounroom* he had seen at a Berlin exhibition in 1923 (fig.37). Lizzitsky, a disciple of Malevich at the Vitebsk art school, had left Russia in 1921 as a covertly official apostle of Constructivism, which was seen as a 'cultural' means to the international dissemination of communist ideas. He was incredibly effective as a theorist-propagandist within progressive western European art and architectural circles during the 1920s, being frenetically active within a network of Constructivist groups and magazines, of which there were no fewer than twenty-seven in

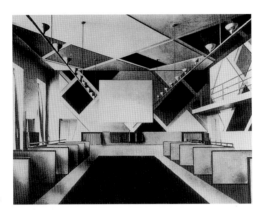

35
Theo van Doesburg

Counter Composition XV 1925

Oil on canvas
50 × 50 (19⅝ × 19⅝)
Museum Sztuki, Poland

36

Photograph of Theo van Doesburg's Café Aubette, Strasbourg 1928

37
El Lizzitsky

Prounroom
(reconstruction)

300 × 300 × 260
(196⅞ × 196⅞ × 102⅜)
Stedelijk van Abbemuseum, Eindhoven

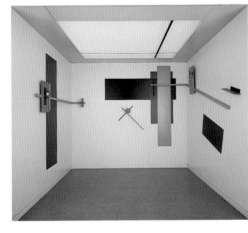

existence in 1925. His *Prounroom* was a three-dimensional realisation of his most original invention, the *Proun*, the word being an abbreviation of the Russian phrase 'Project for the Affirmation of the New'. These designs constituted graphic propositions of an idealised new architecture, the architectonics of buildings that might, with the development of new technologies, soon be possible. They were also concrete images of dynamic relations between two and three dimensions, with the implications of a fourth (in this they continued to reflect his earlier Suprematist ideas): they presented a visionary geometry of the new society.

The tireless Lizzitsky and the restless van Doesburg were both aware of the significance of Dada. Both became friends of its greatest exponent, the Hanover artist Kurt Schwitters, inventor of his own version, *Merz*. (This word was 'stolen', symbolically, from a morally bankrupt system, being adopted from a torn fragment of a poster for the Kommerz und Privatbank he had used in a 1919 collage.) Dada was never a coherent artistic 'movement' with stylistic aspects so much as a series of manifestations and actions by loosely associated artists in different cities, originating in Zurich in 1917. Switzerland, significantly, like post-1917 Russia and the Netherlands, was a neutral country. (Dada 'began' at a satirical night-club, the Café Voltaire; in the same street Lenin was preparing for his return to Russia.) Dada's absolute repudiation of the 'civilisation' that had culminated in

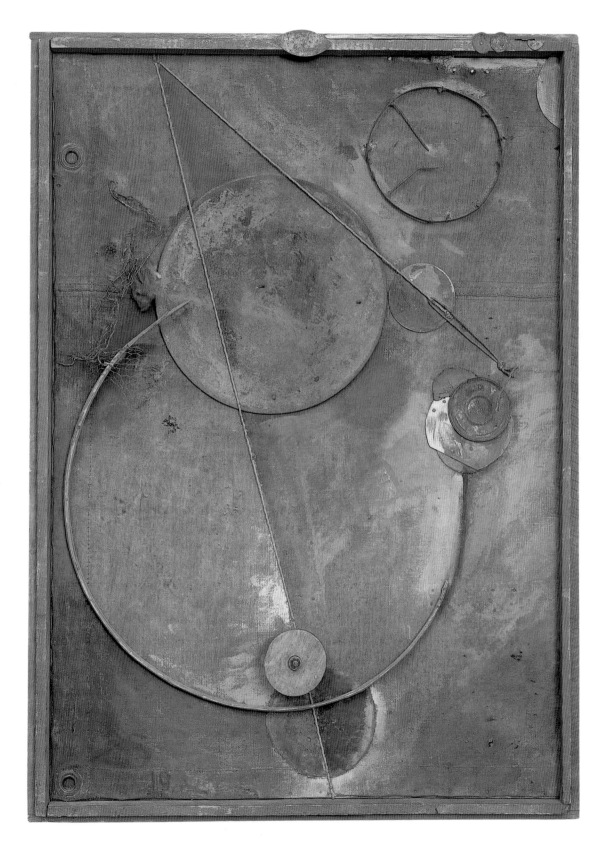

the carnage of the First World War was fundamentally positive, 'the negation of the negation'. In sweeping away the discredited art and culture of the bourgeois epoch, clearing ground for new beginnings, it represented the reverse side of the new coin of Constructivism. There was in fact a great deal of to-ing and fro-ing between Dada and Constructivism in their various manifestations. Van Doesburg himself edited a Dada magazine, *Mecano*, under the pseudonym I.K. Bonset, and organised Schwitters' hilarious Dada tour of Holland in 1922. For his part, Schwitters always proclaimed his commitment to abstraction, and attached to it the same significance as his Constructivist friends. His means and materials, however, were different. He admits into his work the poignancy of the everyday detritus of the world around him: 'even with rubbish one can utter a cry ... The point is to use the broken pieces to create something new'. An early work like *Revolving* 1919 (fig.38) is as radically 'anti-Cubist' in the dynamics of its real presence as a Tatlin construction, and as powerfully cosmic as a

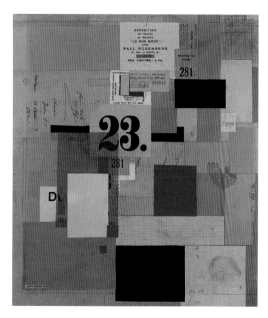

Rodchenko painting. Schwitters assembles its bits of string, wood and tin into an actuality of relations, poetically recycling its humble materials into nothing less than an image of the universe in motion. In *Mz601* 1923 (fig.39) the collage-documentary elements refer ironically to the historical baggage (dealers/ exhibitions/ authentications, etc.) that must be discarded in favour of the purely abstract relations between the *de Stijl*-like red and black rectangles. It is perfectly emblematic of the interlock of Dada and Constructivist ideas. Schwitters was a one-man, post-war artistic revolution. His poetry, like that of the Russian Futurists, returned to the 'concrete' origins of language in pure abstract sound, the phoneme 'as such'. His typography experimented with the abstract signs that are the material components of printed language. This insistence on a (Dada-Constructivist) utilisation of elemental materials placed Schwitters pivotally at the heart of the abstract modernist effort.

Emphasis on the elementary components of visual and plastic language – point, line, plane, colour and materials – was the starting point for studies at the Bauhaus. This great school of design and architecture was founded by Walter Gropius at Weimar in 1919 in the spirit of his slogan 'Art and Technology – a new unity'. In the autumn of 1923 László Moholy-Nagy, a politically radical Hungarian Constructivist who had recently shared a studio with Schwitters in Berlin, was appointed head of the metal workshop and of the Preliminary Course. He quickly became highly influential in the school, turning it in the direction of practical design with an emphasis on the

38
Kurt Schwitters

Revolving 1919

Relief construction of wood, metal, cord, cardboard, wool, wire, leather and oil on canvas
122.7 × 88.7
(48¼ × 34⅞)
The Museum of Modern Art, New York. Advisory Committee Fund

39
Kurt Schwitters

Mz601 1923

Collage
30.3 × 34.7
(12 × 13⅝)
Marlborough Fine Art (London) Ltd

possibilities of mass-production. The year before, Moholy-Nagy had emphasised the primacy of the creative idea over the expressive execution of a work by ordering from a sign factory, by telephone, with precise instructions, three paintings in enamel, *Em 1/2/3* (fig.40), of the same design but in different dimensions. This was a demonstration of Moholy-Nagy's belief in machine technology as an instrument of human expression and social freedom, and of

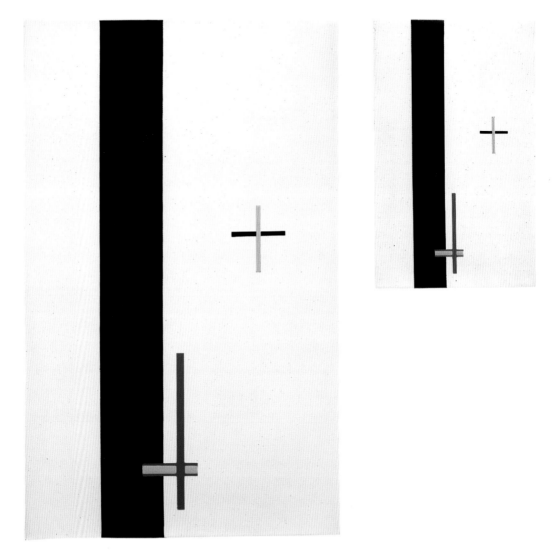

his conviction that mechanical methods (particularly photography) were the means of expression consistent with modernity. Art was a kind of creative technical experimentation. Moholy-Nagy continued, however, to make paintings by hand, sometimes on fabricated supports of plastic or Plexiglas, as well as photographs, plastic-based photomontages and experimental sculptures. In *A20 1927* (fig.41) the effects of painted 'transparency' in translucent superimposed rectangles imaginatively prefigures those of later 'paintings' created purely with light. The black disc that hovers in space recollects Malevich's primal images, but its mechanical precision repudiates any suggestion of a personal, visionary 'given': it is a material part of a painting that is (to paraphrase Le Corbusier) 'a machine for looking at'.

The development and dissemination of Constructivism was based upon the noble idea that after the disasters of the First World War, and the violent convulsions of the Russian Revolution and civil war, art could play a decisive role in the construction of the cultural forms of a new civilisation. The modernist artists, designers and architects of *de Stijl*; Lizzitsky, Moholy-Nagy and the Communist theorists of international Constructivism; the Russian avant-garde artist-teachers in the classrooms of the new Soviet art schools; the

40 A + B
László Moholy-Nagy

Em 2/3 1922

Porcelain enamel on steel
2: 47.5 × 30.1
(18¾ × 11⅞)
3: 24 × 15 (9½ × 6)
The Museum of Modern Art, New York. Gift of Philip Johnson in memory of Sibyl Moholy-Nagy

41
László Moholy-Nagy

A20 1927

Oil on canvas
80 × 95.5
(31½ × 37⅝)
Private Collection.
Courtesy Annely Juda Fine Art, London

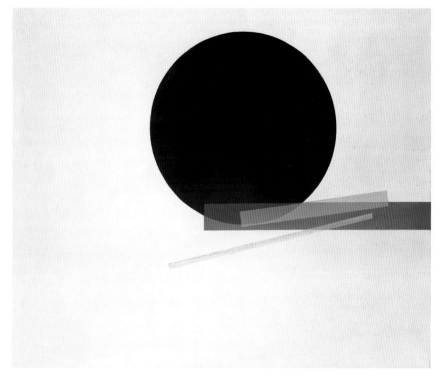

architects, artists and craftsmen of the Bauhaus: almost all subscribed in some measure to this ideal, and to the rhetoric that accompanied it. With the benefit of hindsight and a certain historical realism, we may find ourselves amazed at such optimism, and wonder indeed whether art can ever be an effective agency in the world of actions and events. This is not to question the visionary integrity of some of the most gifted artists of the century, or to deny the intensity of their waking dreams. Their ideas and imaginings are inscribed in their drawings, paintings and constructions; it is this visionary content that moves us so deeply when we encounter their work.

Geometries of the Mind

Naum Gabo left Russia in 1922 on sensing the impending official closure on avant-garde ideas. He was the major progenitor of another kind of constructive abstraction, a 'constructive idea' that comprehends something other than the promise of a new aesthetic directly aligned with the development of radical new social ideals. 'Not to lie about the future is impossible, and one can tell lies at will', he wrote, provocatively, in his famous 'Realistic Manifesto', published

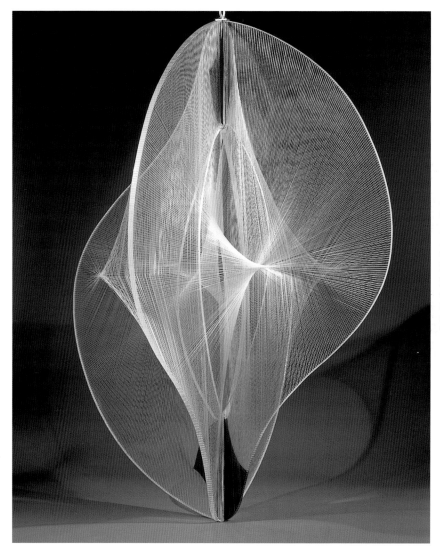

42
Naum Gabo

Linear Construction in Space No.2
Conceived 1949,
fabricated 1972–3

Perspex with nylon monofilament
height: 92 (36¼)
Collection of Nina Williams

in Moscow in 1920. For Gabo, whose formations were in science and engineering, the new art was an expression of the fundamental human creative impulse, also manifest in science and technology, to find an image for what is hidden in the contingent forms of nature. The work of art is not to express individual feelings and thoughts, or propose social or political ideas, but to reveal the invisible inner reality of things. This was 'a totally new attitude towards the artist's task of what to look for … what we perceive with our five senses is not the only aspect of life and nature to be sung about'. The 1920 manifesto had set out his programme with a prophetic lucidity: '*The realisation of our perceptions of the world in the forms of space and time is the only aim of our pictorial and plastic art.*'

Few artists have maintained so coherent a vision as Gabo. A work such as *Linear Construction in Space No.2* (fig.42), conceived in 1949 and fabricated in 1972–3, is recognisably the product of the imagination that conceived of *Column* (fig.43) in Moscow in 1920–1, which was fabricated in 1975. That many of his works have been reconstructed is perfectly consistent with his aims as a sculptor, which had to do with conceptual clarity and impersonal revelation: realisation was merely a matter of the technical construction that made visible the idea. Transparency in both works is a material metaphor-sign for the creative intention to effect this visibility of conceptual structure. These ideas made visible are abstractions (analogous to those of mathematics) from natural phenomena perceived by the eye and conceived by a mind that awaits their occurrence with disciplined expectancy. Their forms may be discovered in sea waves, for example, or pebbles, or in the smoke of a passing train:

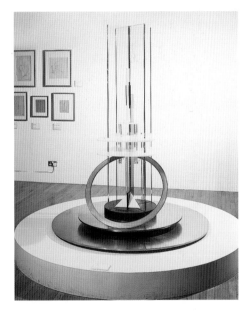

their apparition may be sudden, it may come and vanish in a second, but when they are over they leave with me an image of eternity's duration … sometimes a falling star, cleaving the dark, traces the breath of night on my window glass, and in that instantaneous flash I may see the very line for which I searched in vain for months and months.

These coolly beautiful constructions are created on rigorously geometric principles, abstractions of direction, energy and movement. In *Column*, two transparent vertical planes (panes) intersect centrally at right angles, rising from a circular platform that rests on a series of concentric discs. The planes emerge through a steel ring, which is raised to a dynamic diagonal and is seen necessarily from an angle as an ellipse. In *Linear Construction in Space No.2* the translucent perspex form of a continuous regular arabesque presents the tensioned figure of a wave of energy turning upon an invisible central axis. Both are paradigms of natural order; both are *human* inventions: 'the image of my perception needs an order, and this order is my construction.' For Gabo, and for many of the true geometric abstractionists who followed him, the procedures of art are parallel to those of the mathematician, the scientist, the architect, the engineer and the philosopher.

Art is not mathematics or science, but it may use the findings of both. It has its own technologies, which may be primitive or highly sophisticated, and its purposes may certainly be thought of as philosophical. Art has its own means of communication. In Gabo's words, 'it is more effective through human intuition, through the irrational more than through the rational side of human psychology ... it is operating with man's feelings rather than with man's reason. You cannot reason in a work of art.' An art like that of Gabo's can use any form or shape that is present in the human apprehension of the world. Indeed, it may be the case that 'the square, the circle and the triangle and all the rest of them' – including their volumetric extensions, the cube, the sphere and the cone – were borrowed by the earliest science from art, at a time when the dividing line between those ways of knowing was not clearly drawn. There is no geometry in nature, only in the human mind's apprehension and comprehension of nature. Constructive geometric abstraction has been one of the great and most enduring movements in modern art. It is committed to the invention of image-objects (paintings and constructions) that discover the order that can be discerned in things, an order that can be of many kinds: of colour and tone, of measure and interval, of plane and angle, volume and form, and so on. The incredible variety and richness of this art demonstrates the infinite number of

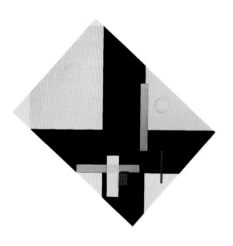

purely abstract ways in which this underlying harmony of the universe can be concretely described. At the end of the 1920s van Doesburg and others called for the term 'concrete' to replace 'abstract', and for the work of art to be a rule-based, self-referring entity, 'entirely conceived and formed by the mind before its execution' with 'absolute clarity' and control; in short, a model of reality.

Friedrich Vordemberge-Gildewart (V-G), like Gabo, arrived quickly at a kind of creative methodology that enabled him to pursue abstract principles with great rigour and clarity. He gave no titles to his works, simply numbering them, thereby implying that each was an item in a potentially unending programme, another way, as it were, of stating what is the case. There is not a work of his that does not exhibit a marvellously self-contained proportion and harmony, inviting analogies, which the artist welcomed as wholly appropriate, to the arts, of music and dance, that depend upon time-based abstract patterns and rhythms. (These analogies suggested new ways to explore kinaesthetic correspondences.) *Composition No.20* 1926 (fig.44) complicates and unsettles Mondrian's device of the 'diamond' (the square rotated by 45 degrees) by setting a grand orthogonal cross against the edges of a diagonal 4 x 3 rectangle, and adding two relief elements, one spherical, the other cubic, to the painted rectangular elements that appear to overlay the black. The over-all effect is to emphasise the top left to lower-right diagonal movement against the stasis of the cross, a contradiction of dynamics quite at odds with Neo-Plastic principles of vertical/horizontal equilibrium. *Composition No.214* 1961 (fig.45) is a late work composed of a right-to-left procession of perfect vertical intervals, complicated by rhythms and counter-

44
Friedrich Vordemberge-Gildewart

Composition No.20
1926

Oil on canvas with two mounted wooden elements
80 × 60 (31½ × 23⅝)
Private Collection.
Courtesy Annely Juda
Fine Art, London

rhythms of colour and tone, texture and design, that work forwards, backwards and diagonally across the plane. It is a piece of the purest visual music, a complex and thrilling analogue of the perpetual rhythms and counter-rhythms of a dance in time. Its measured elements and their relations are mathematically predetermined and controlled.

In 1924 V-G took over the Hanover studio of Lizzitsky, who left behind a portfolio of prints and drawings that were to become for V-G a treasured conceptual and visual resource. Schwitters, based in Hanover, became a close friend, introducing him to Hans Arp and van Doesburg, who, recognising in V-G a kindred spirit at the time of his rupture with Mondrian, enrolled him into *de Stijl*. Such conjunctions of friendship and shared intentions are characteristic of the history of abstraction at every stage, and it is important to

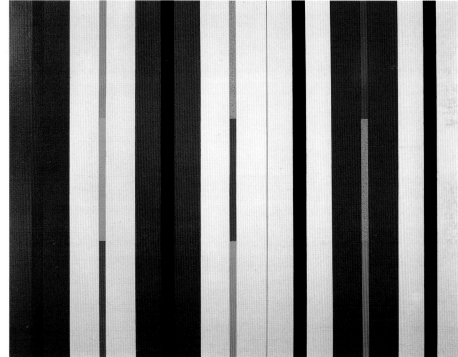

45
Friedrich Vordemberge-Gildewart

Composition No.214
1961

Oil on canvas
80 × 105
(31½ × 41¾)
Private Collection.
Courtesy Annely Juda
Fine Art, London

recognise that there were deep connections between one stage and another in the development of its diverse and overlapping manifestations. Thus, the new mode of conceptual, rule-governed geometric abstraction was conceived at the heart of the utopian project of international Constructivism in the late 1920s. Later, in the 1950s, V-G was to teach at the famous School of Design at Ulm, a kind of latterday Bauhaus, where his colleagues included the Swiss artists Max Bill and Richard Lohse, both of them among the leading post-war theorists of concrete abstraction. Bill proposed a mathematical approach to art; Lohse argued that 'the pictorial field is a structured field' and that colour series in an infinite number of possible permutations provide laws for 'formal expression' (fig.46). Both followed van Doesburg in believing that a work of art is the

objectively 'concrete' expression of the human spirit and that mathematically ordered procedures can discover reality.

It is true, of course, that the mathematical idea is not discovered in the external world but in the human mind: it is a mode of *mental* operation; its systems of signs and messages, of number and conservation, are purely abstract. Geometric Constructivism was in some ways the logical end of those efforts in modern art to make visible the underlying energies and forms that nature hides from the eye, and for which the mind must invent symbolic systems. Many of the most intelligent artists in the later decades of abstraction's epoch have set out to explore the endless possibilities of 'concrete' systematic and serial procedures, in terms of colour and tone, measure and interval, area and volume, number and sequence. Some have based their research

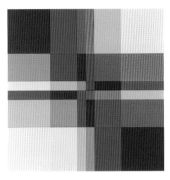

in nature or in the findings of physical sciences, some in colour and its correspondences in sound and the ordered structures of music. For some their formal procedures have been essentially meditative and spiritual, for others purely material and literal. All begin, however, with conceptual determinants that are geometric or mathematical in one way or another, and all work systematically and in series. Among them are the German, Josef Albers, Moholy-Nagy's

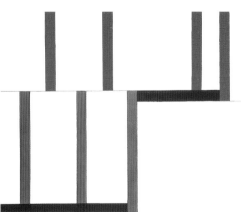

older assistant at the Bauhaus, who became, in the 1930s, an influential teacher at the progressive Black Mountain College in North Carolina; the Polish Constructivists, Wladislaw Strzeminski, Katarzyna Kobro (one of the most original sculptors of the century) and Henryk Stazewski; Georges Vantongerloo (Belgium) (fig.47); Kenneth and Mary

46
Richard Lohse

Six Systematic Colour Series with Horizontal and Vertical Condensation 1955–69

Oil on canvas
150 × 150 (59 × 59)
Richard Paul Lohse Foundation, Zurich

47
Georges Vantongerloo

No.98 2478 Red/135 Green 1936

Oil on wood
57.5 × 56.8
(22⅝ × 22⅜)
Tate

Martin, Michael Kidner, Malcolm Hughes, Anthony Hill, Alan Reynolds (UK); François Morellet, Daniel Buren (France); Charles Biederman, Ad Reinhardt, Sol LeWitt, Donald Judd, Carl Andre (USA); and Victor Vasarely (Hungary). The reader may justly complain that this is nothing more than an (incomplete) list, but it is simply beyond the scope of this little book to attempt a description of the specific procedures and diverse purposes of the many artists whose work is of this kind. Geometric abstraction continues to be a powerful presence in world art; it is perhaps the visual art that has come closest to the pure abstraction of music.

4

FROM POLITICS TO POETICS: POST-WAR ABSTRACTIONS

ACTIONS IN THE ARENA

The creative reaction of many of the early abstract artists to the First World War and to the Russian Revolution was to imagine new political, social and spiritual realities and to invent new forms of art in order to represent them. Art was to assume an actively philosophical agency in the necessary process of cultural and spiritual regeneration. Exactly how art was to play its part in creating the brave new world was a question to which there were many answers. The age demanded, moreover, abstract visual forms capable of response to new relativistic conceptions of reality. To borrow a figure from Wittgenstein, visual analysis of the objective world was like a ladder that could be kicked away once the artist had climbed up it to reach a true understanding of those relational dynamics between things that could only be realised in abstract forms. Many artists thought the new abstract art would be constructively assimilated into the social environment, to become the dynamic aesthetic of *concrete* relations in architecture and design.

   The world looked very different to artists after 1945. Fascism and militarism, economic depression, the material and moral disasters of Communism, the global violence of the Second World War, the revelation of the camps: after these terrible realities the utopian ambitions of the first-generation abstractionists seemed tragically hollow. The progressive artists of the Soviet Union had quickly been condemned to silence and obscurity, or worse; the Bauhaus was closed down in 1933, its artists and architects forced into exile. Of

the pioneer abstractionists, it was pre-1915 Kandinsky whose work most suited the mood of the 1940s, for his had been the most insistent emphasis upon the primacy of feeling, upon 'inner necessity' as the spur to creativity, and upon the faculty of intuition. Kandinsky's painting had the expressive complexity of a vision that was prophetic and apocalyptic rather than utopian and optimistic. He was recognised as the primary inventor of an abstract style that was direct and painterly, personal and disorderly, the historical precursor of what was to be loosely designated 'Abstract Expressionism' or 'action painting'.

These terms, applied generically to the work of abstract painters of the post-war New York School, never served to describe a common style so much as to identify an approach to abstract or near-abstract painting in which the creative emphasis was on the expression of individual sensibility. Such expression necessarily took diverse forms. It was widely claimed, and no doubt believed, that feeling and commitment were translated directly into the 'touch' and brush-stroke that signified the artist's physical and ethical engagement, the unpremeditated 'mark-making' that was the actual evidence of authentic contact with the materials. In Europe the terms *tachisme* (from the French *tache*, meaning 'stroke' or 'blot') and *art autre* ('other art') were coined to describe this kind of free painterly abstraction. The post-war years in Europe and America saw an explosion of such individuated abstractions: the projections not of metaphysical, moral and political ideas so much as of personal ethics and private emotion, mystical and spiritual feeling, psychic experience, dream and myth. Painting was conceived as a heroic and lonely 'action' fraught with risk, but leading, when successful, to the thrilling discovery of an original and revelatory image. This entailed a somewhat naive identification of authenticity with the spontaneous act. 'At a certain moment', wrote the New York critic Harold Rosenberg in 1952, in one of the most famous statements in twentieth-century art criticism, 'the canvas began to appear to one American painter after another as an arena in which to act – rather than as a space in which to reproduce, redesign, analyse or "express" an object, actual or imagined. What was to go on the canvas was not a picture but an event.' Though this may well have been true of certain New York abstractionists, in particular Jackson Pollock, who had been famously photographed and filmed in 1950 by Hans Namuth, working, dance-like, on a floor-based canvas, it was certainly not true of many others.

Even so, according to Alfred Barr, introducing the first comprehensive showing of *The New American Painting* at the Tate Gallery, London, in 1959, these painters did share 'certain strong convictions': 'Many feel their painting is a stubborn, difficult, even desperate effort to discover the "self" or "reality", a struggle to which the whole personality should be recklessly committed … In principle their individualism is as uncompromising as that of the religion of Kierkegaard whom they honour.' This existentialist stance was at one with the prevailing post-war philosophy emanating mainly from Paris, which laid stress upon the agonising imperatives of choice that are concomitant with personal freedom, upon the necessity of commitment to a chosen way of living, and emphatically located the origin of the work of art in the psyche or soul of the artist. The German existentialist Martin Heidegger perfectly summed up the

48
Arshile Gorky
Agony 1947
Oil on canvas
101.6 × 128.3
(40 × 50½)
The Museum of Modern
Art, New York.
A. Conger Fund

identification of the individualistic impulse with the artistic act, which together constituted the creative 'event' that Rosenberg described: 'The artist is the origin of the work. The work is the origin of the artist. Neither is without the other.'

Paradoxically, the commitment demanded might be to the creation of imagery that was 'automatic', that is, arrived at without conscious deliberation, as the consequence of spontaneously arbitrary 'actions' rather than of considered intentions. Its unpremeditated and unpredictable forms were derived, it was supposed, from the individual or collective unconscious, rather in the manner that free association or dreams had been demonstrated by

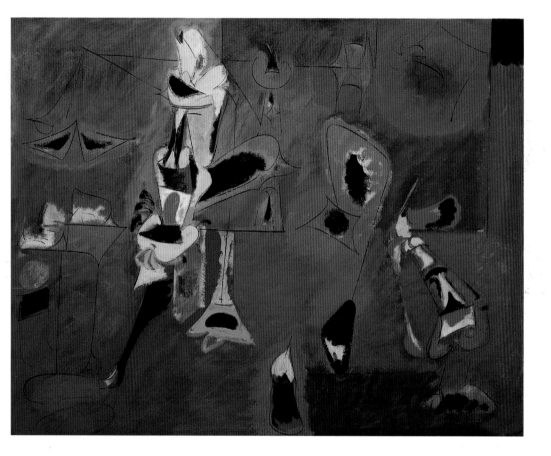

psychoanalysis to bring into view things normally hidden from the conscious mind. The idea of using automatic techniques as a means to generate imagery that might be figurative or abstract derived from Surrealism, and in particular from its principal theoretician, André Breton, who was exiled in New York during the war. Breton had, in fact, originally coined the term 'pure psychic automatism' as the definition of a Surrealist *literary* technique. Automatic practices could be traced in semi-abstract surreal imageries as diverse as those of Joan Miró, Max Ernst, André Masson and Roberta Matta (respectively Spanish, Swiss, French and Chilean: Surrealism in painting was truly

international). Breton was an effective critical champion of these painters, each of whom was a powerfully influential artistic presence, either in person or through important exhibitions in New York during the early and middle 1940s. Painterly automatism, including expressive mark-making and free creation of imaginary forms, was pervasive among those middle-generation New York-based artists, including Jackson Pollock, Mark Rothko, Barnett Newman, Arshile Gorky and Willem de Kooning, who were to become the principal figures of Abstract Expressionism. Much of their work at this time was characterised by biomorphic forms in atmospheric or aqueous space.

Arshile Gorky, the master of this biomorphic style, was the artist whose work most clearly effected the translation of an automatic Surrealist imagery into a subjectively expressive visual poetry. 'Historically', he wrote, 'it has been

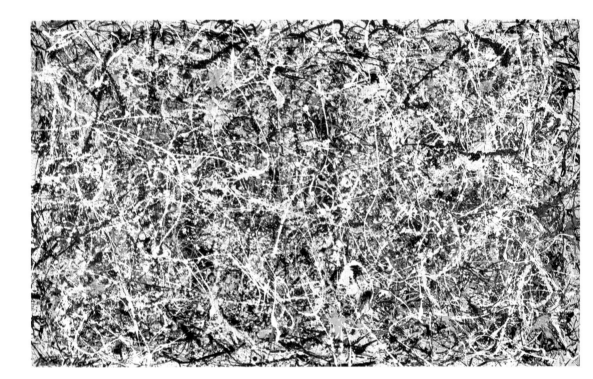

the artist's role to make manifest the beautiful inherent in all the objects of nature and man.' He felt that the Cubists especially had first released the possibilities of such a realisation in the abstract 'magic of space and colour' and that modernism (especially Surrealism) had created the freedoms of abstract expression. Painting was able 'to uncover and interpret life's secrets', which were discovered not in the objectively visible but through the 'mind's eye'. In *Agony* 1947 (fig.48), as in all Gorky's mature paintings, the image is miraculously unfixed. Its linearities never quite describe forms that appear at first sight as objects in space; a space here luminous, here darkened, here transparent and receding, here opaque and planar. It is space that becomes, as we look, pure expressive colour – scarlet, pink, crimson, umber, black – its transitions painful

to the eye. Forms, viscous as those of dreams, dissolve, bleed into the light and dark around them, seem now organic, now mechanical, now suspended and still, now spinning or swinging. Fixing nothing, the image coalesces time and space. Breton dared the viewer of Gorky's paintings to move beyond simple recognitions, to respond to 'the unlimited play of *analogies*' and 'to face the *hybrid* forms in which all human emotion is precipitated'. Gorky's is an art of remembering and evocation, in which joy and pain crystallise into visibility.

The dissolution and dispersal of the object implicit in Gorky's imagery is carried to its absolute extreme in the 'all-over' complexities of Jackson Pollock's paintings of the late 1940s and early 1950s. Here, the agonistic figurative and near-figurative forms of his earlier work (themselves engendered out of a painterly automatism) disappear into an astonishing furore of intricately interweaving straight and curved lines, arabesques, splashes, spillings, stains, splotches, dribbles and whorls. Pollock, above all, exemplified the approach defined by Rosenberg as characteristic of 'the new American painter' who 'no longer approached his easel with an image in his mind; he went up to it with material in his hand to do something to that other piece of material in front of him. The image would be the result of that encounter.' In fact, Pollock had already disposed of the easel itself. In 1947 he described his own dynamic encounter with the materials of his art: 'I prefer to tack the unstretched canvas to the hard wall or the floor … On the floor I am more at ease. I feel nearer, more a part of the painting, since this way I can walk around it, work from the four sides, and literally be *in* the painting … When I am *in* my painting, I'm not aware of what I'm doing.' What was revolutionary about Pollock's automatism, taking it beyond Surrealist experiment, was his use of it to create a purely abstract art on a physical scale unprecedented in modern painting. Its new purpose was not to generate an imagery of unpremeditated objects, but, in eliminating depiction altogether, to create an object itself charged with affective energies.

The rhetoric of creativity that accompanied Abstract Expressionism laid deep stress upon this autonomy of the painting as a object with its own ineluctable dynamic, the outcome of actions whose execution was a creative imperative. 'I have no fears', continued Pollock, 'about making changes, destroying the image, etc., because the painting has a life of its own. I try to let it come through.' In a similar vein, Philip Guston, whose paintings of the 1950s and 1960s have a masterly grace of intuitive touch, wrote: 'Usually I am on a work for a long stretch, until a moment arrives when the air of the arbitrary vanishes and the paint falls into positions that seem destined.' The actions that made such works, visible in painterly traces, marks, strokes and 'figures' (as in 'figure skating'), were seen by Rosenberg to be expressively charged: 'In painting, the primary agency of physical motion … is the line, conceived not as the thinnest of planes, nor as an edge, contour or connective but as a stroke or figure. In its passage on the canvas each such line can establish the actual movement of the artist's body as an aesthetic statement.'

Confronted by a work such as Pollock's tumultuous *Number 1 1949* (fig.49), we are likely to be affected by contradictory tensions. On the one hand, we sense an individual unconscious 'automatically' at one with the cosmic. We

49
Jackson Pollock
Number 1 1949 1949
Enamel and metallic paint on canvas
160×259 (63×102)
Museum of Contemporary Art, Los Angeles. The Rita and Taft Screiber Collection. Given in loving memory of her husband Taft Schreiber by Rita Schreiber

experience the work as the creation of a magical manipulator of energies, an invention of new configurations of 'strokes or figures', the trace of a movement that denies mere 'chance' and is framed and contained by the rectangle of the canvas edge as a skater's might be by the pond edge or the ice-rink fence. Certainly, the painting, created at the height of the artist's powers, is achieved with magisterial aplomb, a magnificently controlled energy. On the other hand, we may find overwhelming evidence of accident and dislocation, and a barely contained picturing of a chaotic potentiality, of anarchic impulses towards a dissolution and disorder that implicitly spread into the infinite space beyond the canvas edge. In either direction, we are contemplating not so much a representation of things in nature as a presentation of the phenomenon of nature itself. The disposition of the paint across the surface has been determined by its energies, becoming an image itself of the ineluctable paradox of nature – its irrepressible proliferation of differentiated forms and rhythms, and its irreversible tendency to entropy.

Many of the paintings that he made in 1947 have titles that clearly indicate Pollock's awareness of the dialectical contradictions, analogous to those in nature, that gives his best work its extraordinary dynamic. It was the year of his crucial breakthrough to the large-scale, so-called 'drip paintings', and the period in which he also adopted the free-flowing media – aluminium and enamel paints – appropriate to his new technique. *Galaxy*, *Comet*, *Reflection of the Big Dipper* and *Phosphorescence*, for example, reflect his subjective identification with the natural phenomena of the ordered cosmos; *Lucifer*, *Alchemy*, *Sea Change* and *Full Fathom Five* hint at a hubristic claim to the Prospero-like powers of the magus over a world in continuous entropic flux. Pollock achieved fame as the the temperamental, angst-ridden artist as tragic hero. Between 1948 and 1951 numbers and dates seemed sufficient as titles: the works spoke for themselves. The paintings of Pollock most indicative of his original genius are those whose scale overwhelms and engulfs the viewer, filling the visual field with energy materialised, inducing the sensation of being 'in the arena' of painting, as the artist was in its making. With these works effect is all: the spectator becomes a protagonist, with a wonderful freedom of engaged imagination. Pollock's immense artistic reputation rests essentially upon the large paintings produced in the few years indicated. The smaller abstract paintings are fascinating and sometimes beautiful exercises in his disctinctive individual manner; with the exception of a small number of remarkably powerful symbolic paintings of the early 1940s, most of his figurative work remains interesting chiefly because he painted it.

The best paintings of Barnett Newman, whose temperament was of a kind quite different from that of Pollock, also work through effects of scale, painterly plenitude and figurative emptiness. Newman, thoughtful, conscientious, intellectual and mystical, was a formidable and influential rhetorician in the critical promotion of 'the new movement' in painting, which he described as early as 1945 as 'subjective abstraction'. Newman was at that time anxious to dissociate such work (his own and that of Pollock, Rothko and Adolph Gottlieb) from Surrealism, with its 'mundane' concern with 'the human psyche' and the 'mystery of [the artist's] own personality', in order to emphasise

its higher, symbolic purposes. The new art was 'concerned with the sublime ...
It is a religious art which through symbols will catch the basic truth of life
which is its sense of tragedy'. Like his friends, in the late 1940s he liberated
himself from the dream-like biomorphic symbolism of his earlier work to
develop a distinctive and influential, purely abstract style of his own. This was
characterised by large fields of undifferentiated colour, demarcated only by the
canvas edges or by the hard edge of an abutting field, or separated by a thin
vertical strip (the famous trademark 'zip'). He adamantly continued to insist,
however, on the tragic symbolic *content* of his painting.

Newman disclaimed any link between his own work and that of the first-
generation geometric abstractionists. His generation had virtually no first-hand
knowledge of Malevich, and thought, erroneously, of the great Russian's art as
strictly geometric. He knew Mondrian's work, but regarded his 'Neo-Plastic'
prescriptions as a formalistic dogma. For Newman the creation of the colour
field in his own art was an act of revelation achieved through unconstrained
colour rather than the idealist proposal of a desirable order. His painting was

50
Barnett Newman

Who's Afraid of Red,
Yellow and Blue? III
1957

Oil on canvas
245 × 543
(96½ × 213¾)
Stedelijk Museum,
Amsterdam

an attempt to 'discover a new image' with no basis in 'the geometry principles of
World War I'. 'Only an art of no-geometry', he declared, 'can be a new
beginning'. In spite of these protestations, Newman's vertical juxtapositions of
colour fields are, of course, essentially geometric arrangements, and he never
sought to escape from the geometry of the canvas. (Some late paintings were
actually made on canvases stretched as regular triangles.) As with Pollock,
however, it is the overwhelming physical and affective presence, in his case of a
monumental radiance, that defines the true originality and distinction of
Newman's greatest work. The declared intention of the large paintings is to
induce transcendental feelings of awe and wonder at the miracle of existence.
The narrow vertical in Newman's work may be a symbol for the heroic figure,
or suggest an aperture onto darkness or light; the expansive colour field is a sign
for the infinity of space and light. In its striving to create the effect of a sublime
limitlessness his work differs profoundly from that of the father-figure of his
mature art, Mondrian, whose idealising geometry and black lines, according to
Newman, strictly delimit the planes of primaries, reducing those colours to a

'dogmatic idea-didact'. In the defiantly magisterial series of 1957, *Who's Afraid of Red, Yellow and Blue? III* (fig.50), he explicitly challenged the domestic-scaled propositions of Mondrian's Neo-Plasticism. These works are not a revision of Mondrian on a grand scale: they proceed from quite different premises.

Mark Rothko also arrived at his own style, absolutely abstract, at the end of

the 1940s. He continued thereafter to produce variations of a characteristic, apparently simple image in which two or more soft-edged, roughly rectangular shapes, like clouds or bars of colour-light, hover parallel to the edges of the canvas, never quite touching them, as if floating in space (fig.51). Even in reproduction, this is a compelling device, having an iconic frontality, like an

abstract face. In the presence of the real thing, however, you become slowly aware of an affective complexity. This is partly a function of Rothko's consummate play with colour, with dynamics of tone and hue, translucence and opacity, wash and saturation of the most extraordinary subtlety and beauty, partly of the illusion of light or darkness emanating from the centred shapes to become a luminous or tenebrous shimmer at their edges. (This effect of blurred edge is anticipated in Rozanova's *Green Stripe* (fig.5), as is the frontal iconic affect.) It is also to do with spatial ambiguities, with relations of shape and colour in which nothing seems determined and settled, and with disconcerting surface complications that draw attention away from the reality

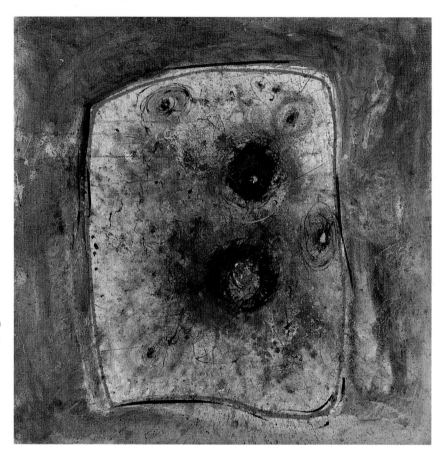

51
Mark Rothko

Red-Brown, Black, Green, Red 1962

Oil on canvas
206 × 193.5
(81⅛ × 76⅛)
Fondation Beyeler, Basel

52
Wols (Wolfgang Schülze)

Painting 1944–5

Oil on canvas
81 × 81.1
(31⅞ × 31⅞)
The Museum of Modern Art, New York. Gift of D. and J. de Menil Fund

of the image to the actuality of the painting-as-painting. Rothko made large works, but rarely on the mural scale that offers a phenomenological substitute for nature. His paintings operate, rather, upon the meditative eye, demanding sustained contemplation. Rothko claimed that his pictures were 'realistic' and expressed 'basic human emotions – tragedy, ecstasy, doom', and protested that to be 'moved only by their colour relationships' was 'to miss the point'. The acknowledged power of his paintings, nevertheless, lies precisely in the freedom of response they grant the spectator, a response that may have many levels of meaning. The beautiful drama of their forms and colours encourages reverie,

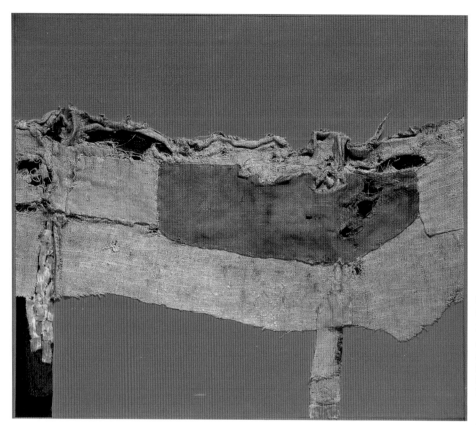

53
Alberto Burri

Sacking and Red 1954

Acrylic and hessian
collage on canvas
86.4 × 100.3
(34 × 39½)
Tate

54
Jean Fautrier

*Hostages on a Black
Ground* 1946

Etching on laid paper
24.2 × 32.7
(9½ × 12⅞)
Tate

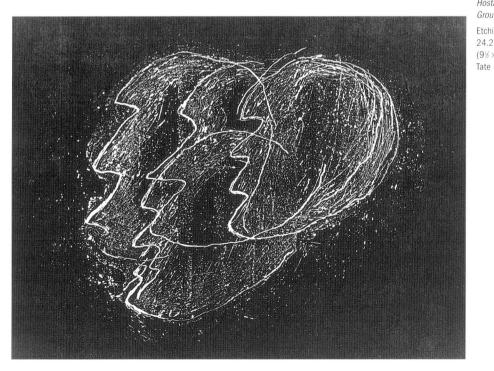

and who can prescribe the particular workings of the individual imagination?

In allowing for the spectator's imaginative (re-)creation of the work, Abstract Expressionist painting extended the subjective freedoms won by the first generation of abstractionists and by the Analytic Cubism of Braque and Picasso. It effected a crucial shift in emphasis, from a demand for conscious engagement in political, philosophical and spiritual programmes, or for critical reflection on perceptual/conceptual propositions, to an invitation to poetic experience of emotional, spiritual and existential states. Many post-war European abstract artists also found their way to a distinctive kind of poetic abstraction. Its scale was less expansive than that of the New York painters – materials in Europe were scarce and expensive – but in its smaller arenas the action was conducted at levels of extreme emotional intensity. In the late 1940s the German-born, Paris-based Wols acquired a legendary reputation as the model of the authentic existentialist artist, the small, sometimes miniature, scale of his work intensifying its air of desolate alienation (fig.52). Others artists in that troubled time, such as the Italian Alberto Burri, the Spaniard Antoni Tàpies and the Frenchman Jean Fautrier, created, like Wols, an imagery that drew directly on the rough, pitted textures of the damaged and soiled urban fabric of post-war Europe (figs.53–4). In the darker mood of a devastated continent, these so-called *informel* artists committed themselves to *un 'art autre'*, to subjective abstraction as the means to the exploration of sombre inner experience, and to the expression of existential anguish. In the work of many other European artists, such as Picasso, Jean Dubuffet, Francis Bacon and Alberto Giacometti, the spirit of the age was answered by an agonised figuration.

THE RETURN OF NATURE

Many abstract artists have claimed a visual autonomy for their work, believing it to create the dynamically self-contained occasion for an aesthetic, emotional and mental response that is immediate to the painting itself rather than to a *picture* evocative of things in the world at large. However, a great deal of abstract art, as we have seen, seems to retain or contain references, of one sort or another, to the external world. These might be found in disguised or distorted forms, in hints and suggestions of figures, or in passages open to visual interpretation. They might, in more general terms, be discovered in accidental or unavoidable resemblances to natural phenomena: to colour in nature, for example, as the sky is blue, fields green, clouds white or grey; or in configurations of lines and strokes, marks, stipples, impasto, etc. that remind the viewer of atmospheric effects, of calm or turbulent weather, of the shimmer of light on water or the swirl of a marine current, and so on. They might be found in shapes that bring to mind the elemental forms of sun and moon, rocks and trees, fruit, flowers and birds, the human figure, or such architectural and mechanical objects as houses, boats and aeroplanes.

Recognising this, and embracing its implications, a great many abstract artists in the period after the Second World War set aside the metaphysical and utopian ambitions of their great predecessors and determined to make art that avowedly reflected in some way their immediate experience of the phenomenal

world. These artists found inspiration in diverse sources: in the faceted indeterminacies of Analytic Cubism and in the pictorial architectonics of its Synthetic phase; in the poetic universe of Paul Klee; in the arbitrary colourism and abstract-figurative formal invention of Matisse; in the very different 'all-over' abstract surface complexities of the late works of both Claude Monet and Pierre Bonnard; and of course in both non-geometric colour fields and free painterly abstractions. Their efforts were to effect a synthesis of abstraction and representation.

The work of Willem de Kooning, one of the most passionately committed of the American action painters, exemplifies that synthesis. In *Door to the River* 1960 (fig.55), one of a series of paintings made in the late 1950s and early 1960s, the emphatically spontaneous brushstrokes declare the gestures that have made them, giving the painting a thrilling physical immediacy, its surface alive with incident and contrast, and absolutely 'present' in the space of the spectator. At the same time its structures of colour and texture create complex spatial ambiguities, similar to those we have experienced in Cubist painting, which summon into imagined visibility the actualities of weather and light in a landscape, with things near (the 'door', a foreground path, a fence?) and things far (the 'river', the sky?). Nothing is definite in this image, all is allusive and atmospheric; it is not a depiction of a place and its objects but a reality reconstituted and represented in paint. Whether such a door or river ever existed 'in the world' is not at issue; paint has brought them into being as imaginable possibilities, and only this painting could have made possible the constructions we put upon it. The low-key poetic title, like those of others in the series – *Suburb in Havana*, *September Morn*, *Pastorale* – suggests a particular subject, but the painting's dynamic evocation of the world transcends specific reference: for the spectator it is itself the place and moment of vital experience.

De Kooning, born in Rotterdam, was highly conscious of his great Dutch predecessors. Thinking of van Gogh, and remembering the strictures of Mondrian's 'abstract-real' painter, we may quite properly find in the capricious and fantastic forms of his paintings the 'tragic beauty' of 'natural reality'. Finding himself in a violently contingent world, de Kooning sought no consoling equilibrium in art: 'Art never seems to make me peaceful or pure', he wrote; ' I do not think of art ... as a situation of comfort.' Different temperaments experience the world in different ways, and find the means to its expression – the expression of the world – in modes distinctively appropriate to subjective realities. Individual styles develop out of these differences. Poetic abstraction (as Gorky recognised so early) has been able to draw upon the great diversity of modernist experiment, figurative, Surrealist and abstract, with an unprecedented freedom, and without constraints of ideological principle beyond those implicit in the demand for 'authenticity' or truth to personal experience. The 'world experienced' by painters includes paintings by others. If there is an Expressionistic vehemence in de Kooning's brushwork, there is also, as I have implied, a pictorial structure that derives from his assimilation of Cubism, a set of formal relations on the work's surface that is analogous to those between things in the world. '"Cubism" once discovered could not be undiscovered and ... has been absorbed into human experience as we know it

today', wrote the British painter Ben Nicholson in 1955. 'Painting today, and it was Cézanne who made the first vital moves, and Picasso and Braque – and Mondrian – who carried the discovery further, is a bird on the wing.'

Nicholson's own painting effects a synthesis of Cubist visual complexity and the ordered calm of the late Mondrian. His work and that of Nicolas de Staël, another highly influential European painter of quite different temperament,

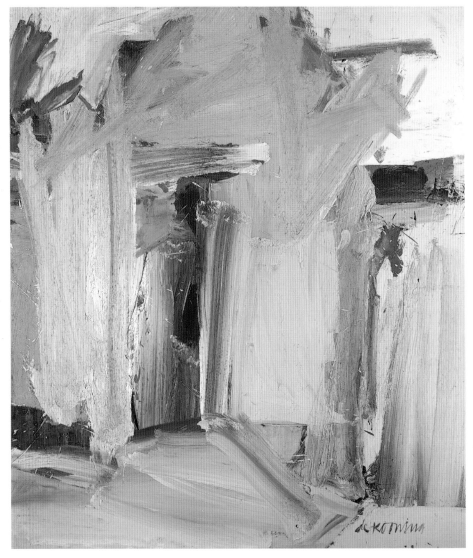

55
Willem de Kooning

Door to the River 1960

Oil on canvas
203.2 × 177.8
(80 × 70)
Whitney Museum of
American Art, New York.
Purchased with funds
from the friends of the
Whitney Museum of
American Art

demonstrate in contrasting ways the enduring power of the Cubist vision, admitting into avowedly 'abstract' paintings traces of the referential, deliberate reflections and refractions of the world extraneous to the painting itself. Colour, shapes and surface textures survive from a given subject as a kind of memory; the spectator is free to imagine a way back to the objective world. 'The poetic experience of [an event in nature] can only be realised in painting

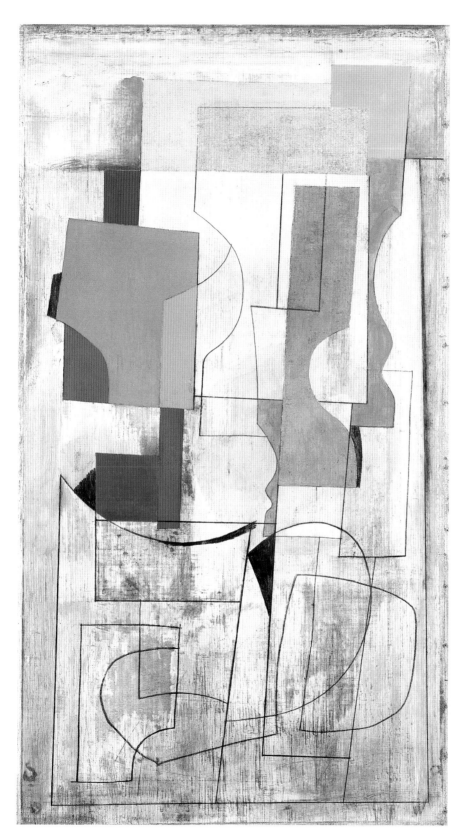

56
Ben Nicholson
Feb 28–53 (vertical seconds) 1953
Oil on canvas
75.6 × 41.9
(30⅛ × 16½)
Tate

57
Nicholas de Staël
Figure at the Seashore 1952
Oil on canvas
161.5 × 129.5
(63⅝ × 51)
Kunstsammlung
Nordrhein-Westfalen,
Düsseldorf

58
Hans Hofmann
Pompeii 1959
Oil on canvas
214 × 132.7
(84¼ × 52¼)
Tate

by an equivalent, out of the painter's total experience, when it can become all things to all men.' *Feb 28–53 (vertical seconds)* 1953 (fig.56), like many of Nicholson's paintings, retains glimpses of a still-life arrangement (the curved contours of jugs, mugs, vases), moments of naturalistic colour (the pale blue of sky seen through a window) and texture (the scraped and stained support like a scrubbed tabletop), but its realisation as an autonomous 'poetic experience' transcends its origins in the observation of nature. It works upon the eye (and mind) as a musical canon might upon the ear (and mind) by purely abstract qualities of rhythmic repetition, reprise and reversal, tonal variation within a distinctive key, and harmony.

The rich chromatic chords of de Staël's *Figure at the Seashore* 1952 (fig.57) are aspects of another Cubistic music, more plangent, more openly sensational. For de Staël, the action of painting was a concatenation of seeing, knowing and transformation: those thick blocks of paint laid with such conviction onto the canvas with a palette knife are elemental abstractions of the forms and colours

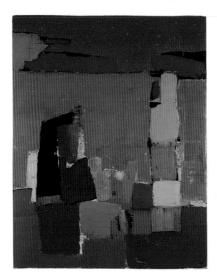 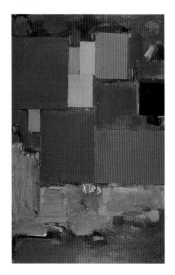

of nature observed. In painting 'two things matter', he wrote: 'the force and intensity of the touch and that of the thought behind it … And what can one do if by dint of burning up the retina of one's eye on the "shattering blue" as [René] Char puts it, one ends up by seeing the sea red and the sand violet …' That essentialising economy, of simplified shapes and pure arbitrary colour, is Matisse's special gift to poetic abstraction. It was a salutary principle for artists on both sides of the Atlantic, as diverse of temperament and intention as Milton Avery, Hans Hofmann (fig.58), Alexander Calder, Anthony Caro, Bridget Riley and Patrick Heron (figs.59–60).

Carried to a doctrinaire and reductive extreme, it led in the 1960s to the orthodoxies of what was dubbed 'post-painterly abstraction': flat, stained fields or veils of synthetic colour, and inexpressive, 'hard edge' parallel stripes and concentric circles, such as in the early paintings of Frank Stella or the work of Morris Louis and Kenneth Noland. It was an art that denied texture, tonality and modelling in fictional space in favour of the purely optical: 'what you see is

what you see'. Even such strictly formal devices, however, for all their apparent autonomy as perfectly flat images of nothing but themselves, cannot exclude memories of atmospheric light, of horizons and heavenly bodies: the mind naturally seeks such resemblances.

There is in de Staël's paintings a powerful impulse to architectonic structure that holds in check the expressive vehemence of the paint stroke and gives his canvasses a monumental poise. In this aspect his work, like Nicholson's and Riley's, exemplifies one of two principal tendencies involved in the conception and making of those poetic abstractions that have their origins in the experience of nature, a nature that includes the objects and experiences of the man-made, the domestic, the agricultural, the architectural, the life of the city. This principle informs painting in which the experience of the phenomenal world is distilled to a kind of stillness, transformed into an image of poise or

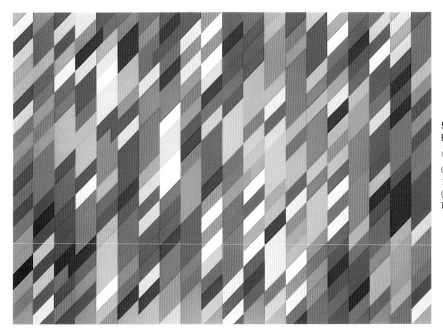

59
Bridget Riley

Nataraja 1993

Oil on canvas
165.1 × 227.7
(65 × 89⅝)
Tate

calm. Implicit always in such art are the dialectical tensions that maintain an instant of stasis; there is a sense of energies held in poise, of potential destruction of this momentary balance, lending to its dissolution and the redistribution of its constituent elements. A moment of reality (life is a succession of such moments) is crystallised for our contemplation, held in what the French philosopher Gaston Bachelard calls 'a lucid tranquillity'.

The other modality of abstraction, perfectly exemplified by the painting of de Kooning and of Heron, is that of a kinetic representation of the world experienced as flux, as a complex of sensations in which it is impossible to hold anything still. In this thrilling place our sensorium is assailed by the teeming facts of the actual, and their poetic realisations have the flickering inconstancy of fire. Painting of this kind revels in the evanescence of the elements, in the ceaseless play of light and shadow, in intensities of colour, in vivid creatures, in

60
Patrick Heron

Horizontal Stripe
Painting: November
1957 – January 1958
1957–8

Oil on canvas
274.3 × 154.8
(108 × 61)
Tate

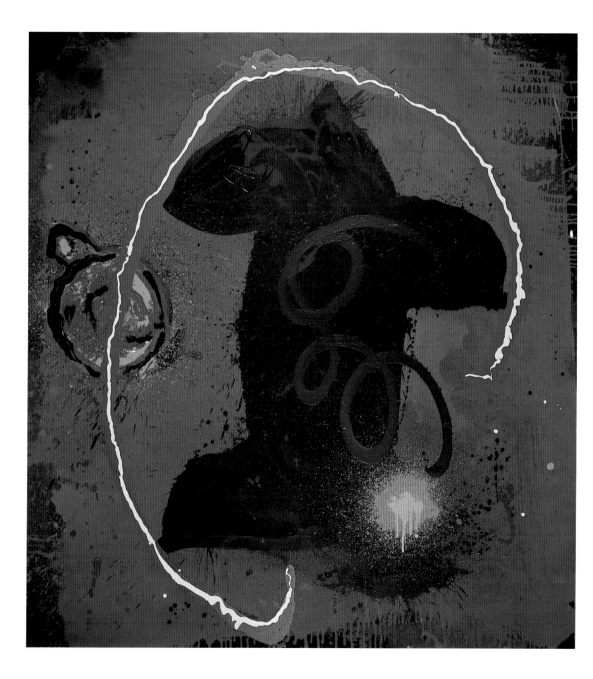

the rhythms of free dance and the dissonances of jazz. If the art of an achieved poise is a function of reverie, of daydream, then this art of perpetual movement has its equivalence in night-time dreaming, and is characterised by a swirling viscosity, an oneiric vagueness of forms. It is not without its own beautiful precisions. 'The poet of vagueness', wrote Italo Calvino, 'can only be the poet of exactitude, who is able to grasp the subtlest sensations with eyes and ears and quick, unerring hands ... the search for the indefinite becomes the observation of all that is multiple, teeming, composed of countless particles.' John Hoyland's *Black Something* 1990 (fig.61) may be taken as the signature of such a poet-artist: it presents a magisterial ideogrammatic arabesque, a quick image of helical energy caught within an arc of electrical light: a sign for the painter's art that can magically call into being cosmic forms, manifestations of the sheer energy that informs the living universe. In 1978 Hoyland wrote: 'Paintings are not to be reasoned with, they are not to be understood, they are to be recognised. They are an equivalent to nature, not an illustration of it; their test is in the depth of the artist's imagination.' To which we might add that their true test is in the answering imagination that we bring to them, that transforms them into an aspect of our own reality in nature.

61
John Hoyland

Black Something 1990

Acrylic on cotton
100 × 93
(39⅜ × 36⅝)
Private Collection

FULLNESS AND EMPTINESS

The extravagant actualities of the phenomenal world may be represented in an abstract imagery that holds reality in the architectonic stasis of the frozen moment or one that signifies its kinetic furore. But any abstract art that lays claim to express the experience of nature must acknowledge in some way or another its multifarious and changing colours, shapes and forms, its never-ceasing dynamics. Such an art must have *a subject*. Hoyland has given us a comically random (and marvellously precise) list of his own 'subjects': among the things in nature to which 'equivalents' are discovered in the fantasy of his paintings are 'shields, masks, tools, artefacts, mirrors, Avebury Circle, swimming underwater ... views from planes, volcanoes, mountains, waterfalls, rocks, graffiti, stains, damp walls, pavements, puddles, the cosmos inside the human body ... being drunk, sex, music, relentless rhythm ... tropical light, the oceanic light ... dawn, sunsets, trees, flowers ... ' In a famous statement made as early as 1943 Rothko and his friend Gottlieb declared (in defence of the semi-abstract symbolism of their recent work): 'There is no such thing as good painting about nothing. We assert that the subject is crucial and only that subject matter is valid that is tragic and timeless.' So far from retracting this when his work had become purely abstract, Rothko chose to emphasise the point. 'The whole of man's experience becomes his model,' he said in 1958, and among the 'ingredients' of his art he listed a 'preoccupation with death ... Sensuality, the basis for being concrete about the world ... Tension: conflict or desire ... a few grams of the ephemeral ... '

A powerful idea informing much of the abstract art of the last forty years or so has been, then, that it constitutes a heroic engagement with the environment of human action, that its principal purpose is to encompass the objects and events of the world we inhabit and to express something of our complex, amazed and troubled responses to them. During the 1950s, at a time when that idea provided for the majority of artists their most compelling motive, the enduring claims of an opposing philosophy were raised in the work of a number of painters. Against an art full of sound and fury signifying so much, an art embroiled with the matter and energy of things in time and space, these artists created a disengaged art that sought to signify nothing, to be nothing but its own thing, devoid of reference, avoiding expression. To the ambition that fuelled actions in the arena of abstract expression, or the anguished existentialism of 'informal' abstractions, they opposed a contemplative composition of the spirit. To the sensuous revelation of phenomenal realities and the celebration of natural plenitude they presented a material emptiness, an art without content: 'PAINTING AS "NOT AS A LIKENESS OF ANYTHING ON EARTH."'

Ad Reinhardt, who coined this emphatic slogan, was a sophisticated and eloquent spokesman for this counter–tendency. Born and based in New York, and a friend of Abstract Expressionist contemporaries in the city, he produced writings notable for their apothegmatic wit and caustic intelligence. To de Kooning's 'Art never seems to make me peaceful or pure,' he replied: 'Art never seems to make me vulgar or violent.' His response to the famous statement of Rothko and Gottlieb was equally perverse: 'There is no such thing as a good painting about something.' The idea of art as an active involvement in the endless evanescence of things elicited from him a soliloquy that is Hamlet-like in its scrupulous deliberation:

62
Ad Reinhardt
Abstract Painting No. 5
1962
Oil on canvas
152.4 × 152.4
(60 × 60)
Tate

To be part of things or not to be part or having been part of things as they've become, to part from that part that was part of things as they are or not to part? … Some claim to represent nature, hell on earth, sick society, inner turmoil, wild beasts and things as they are. May not one side of me speak up for the side of the angels?'

The angels, as we know, are not of this world. And other-worldliness is a quality of the art that Reinhardt sought to define, and to create in line with its definition.

The great works of Reinhardt's late maturity, the so-called 'Black Paintings' of the mid-1950s and early 1960s in which he finally eliminated the chromatic blues and reds of earlier paintings with similar formats, are mysterious and highly charged works, but their strangeness and affective energy is not that of analogy or equivalence with anything in nature. Indeed, it is the unavoidably *referential* nature of colour that necessitated its elimination from these works. By a paradox, only in the negation of blackness – the definitive absence of light and of colour – can the light that was never seen 'on earth' be suggested, the light that must be perceived in the darkness of these paintings. The absolute, cruciform symmetry of their design ('*no composition*') traced in divisions of the most minimal (and unreproducible) variations of blackness, almost invisible to the spectator, is geometric in the way of Tantric diagrams: intended, that is, to divert attention from any *natural* contingency. It is an iconic device demanding an intensity of attention that can induce a state close to the mesmerised, rather than the proposition of a mathematical, conceptual ideal. This icon – 'a square (*neutral, shapeless*) canvas, five feet wide, five feet high, as high as a man, as wide as a man's outstretched arms' (the most extreme abstraction of the Vitruvian ideal) –

may be seen, Reinhardt stated, 'as device, diagram, emblem, frame, game, sign, spectacle'. He elaborated: 'Device as empty. Diagram as dead. Emblem as archetype. Frame as (of) mind. Sign as forecast. Spectacle as invisible.' Its purpose is to serve as the object of a sustained regard, nothing more, and nothing less. Each is complete in itself, referring to nothing outside itself: in this regard, the 'Black Paintings' depart finally from the traditional purpose of the icon image, which was to act as the reminder of the subject of meditation. What the beholder of *Abstract Painting No.5* 1962 (fig.62) may experience, in time, is the ecstatic *nothing* that is an answer to the question: what does it mean? These were the 'first paintings which cannot be misunderstood'.

Where Malevich's bituminous square – *pitch* black – was an abstract *image* of compacted energies, physical and spiritual, Reinhardt's *diagram* demanded to be

contemplated as the negation of everything it was not, including all species of abstraction itself. It was art as

the most extreme, ultimate reaction to, and negation of the (cubist, Mondrian, Malevich, Albers, Diller) tradition of abstract art, and previous paintings of horizontal bands, vertical stripes, blobs, scumblings, bravura, brushwork, impressions, impastos, sensations, impulses, pleasures, pains, ideas, imaginings, imagings, visions, shapes, colours ... accidents, actions ... spontaneities, ready-mades ... meanings, forms of any traditions of pure, or impure, abstract-art traditions, my own and every one else's.

This cumulative comic denial is in deliberate response to the cosmic rhetoric and self-dramatising heroics that have so often characterised the utterance of abstract artists from Malevich onwards. 'Art is art-as-art' Reinhardt wrote. 'Everything else is everything else. Art-as-art is nothing but art. Art is not what is not art.'

Yves Klein, the French artist who died, aged only thirty-four, in 1962, was, like Reinhardt, deeply interested in Far Eastern methods of meditative action (he studied in Japan to become a Judo master). He was an inspired maker of texts and a consummate self-publicising *provocateur*. His gift, in these latter respects, was for a compelling, deadpan ambiguity, which, at once comic and solemn, asserted his (perfectly serious) claim to pre-eminence as an artist-philosopher of the Void. Writing of his exhibition in Paris of that title (*Le vide* 1958), in which nothing was to be 'seen' but the empty space. 'My paintings are now invisible, and I would like to show them in a clear and positive manner,' he declared.

The immaterial blue colour shown at Iris Clert's [Gallery] in April had in short made me inhuman, had excluded me from the world of tangible reality; I was an extreme element of society who lived in space and who had no means of coming back to earth. Jean Tinguely saw me in space and signalled to me in speed to show me the last machine to take to return to the ephemerality of material life.

The 'unfortunate but great Malevich' also visited him in space, where Klein 'was already, since always, owner, inhabitant, or rather co-owner and coinhabitant.' His escape from 'the phenomenology of time' permitted him to say 'honestly and calmly, that Malevich painted a still life after one of my monochrome paintings'.

In the same year (1955–6) in which Reinhardt made the first of his 'Black Paintings' Klein had initially realised his own totally monochromatic paintings. He claimed to have invented them conceptually as early as 1947, and from the outset he referred to them as 'Propositions', emphasising thereby that their physical actuality was merely the means to the presentation of a philosophical or spiritual idea. The monochrome was to be apprehended as an effective *presence* signifying in its shimmering oneness an absolute *absence* of effect. It was a thing merely for the want of a nothing, intended to create, in the optical sensation of invisibility, an experience of cosmic indivisibility. Klein's first exhibitions, in Paris in 1956, were of monochromes in different colours – greens, reds, yellows, purples, blues, oranges. He was disappointed to observe the public at the private view, 'prisoners of a pre-conceived point of view', responding to their inter-relations of colour as components of 'a decorative polychromy'. 'It was then', he wrote later, 'that I remembered the colour blue, the blue of the sky in Nice that was at the origin of my career as a monochromist'.

63
Yves Klein
IKB 79 1959
Paint on canvas on wood
139.7 × 119.7 × 3.2
(55 × 47⅛ × 1¼)
Tate

For his next show, in Milan in 1957, Klein arrived at his own unique solution to the problem of securing contemplative attention to the works in isolation, by which each would be realised as a proposition, in itself, of the absolute reality of infinite space, the very infinity that optically creates the blue of the sky. He invented a totally synthetic, non-naturalistic, non-referential blue, a version of ultramarine known from then on as International Klein Blue (IKB) (fig.63). Its pigmented powder is secured without an oil fixative, and its granular surface of dense blue resonates on the eye like the vibration of the monotone symphony, also first conceived by Klein in 1947, which, in his own words, 'consists of one single, continuous, long-drawn-out "sound": it has no beginning nor end, which creates a dizzy feeling, a sense of aspiration, of a sensibility outside and beyond time.' The tone of his claim for priority is typical: 'The glaring obviousness of my paternity of monochromy in the twentieth century is such that even if I myself were to fight hard against that fact I should probably never manage to rid myself of it.'

A distinguished older artist, already internationally famous when he

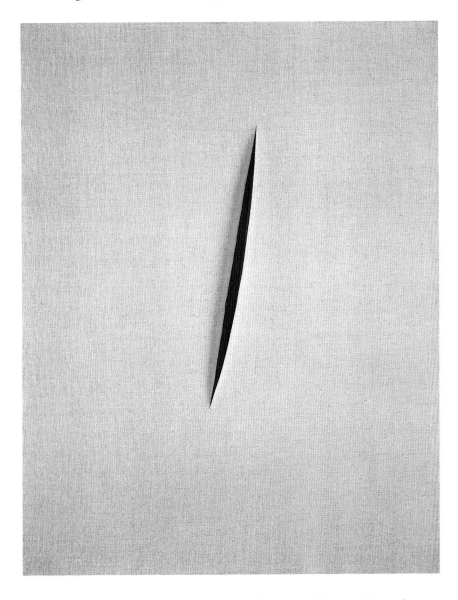

64
Lucio Fontana

*Spatial Concept
(Waiting)* 1960

Canvas
93 x 73
(36⅝ x 28¾)
Tate

encountered, and greatly admired, Klein's work at the Milan exhibition, the Italian Lucio Fontana had for some years made his own monochrome paintings. These were mostly off-white, cream and pale ochre, their surfaces punctured with constellations of troubling small, rough holes, as if proposing by way of an extreme opposition (black holes, pale ground) the image of the stars in the infinite night sky. In 1958, however, Fontana performed for the first time an extraordinary, radical act: he cut, with a stanley knife, a clean incision into a plain and immaculately painted monochrome surface. The *tagli* — slit canvases — have an extreme simplicity and economy, especially those single-slit *Spatial Concept* paintings subtitled *Attesa (Waiting)* (fig.64). These unforgettable images, ambiguous and elegant, are susceptible to a multiplicity of readings and responses. They deeply surprised those who first saw them, and were interpreted by some as menacing, even violent, and sexually charged.

Fontana's own emphasis was always upon the *spatial* aspect, and its spiritual connotations, upon perforation and incision as the means to extend the object towards infinity, to open it up to actual space behind and beyond, with all the metaphysical implications this might suggest. That behind the slits in the *Attese* series Fontana has attached strips of black gauze means that the dark space they open on to is actually an illusionistic phenomenon of the same categorical order as perspectival space. The device renders the black space metaphorical, a quality quite absent from Reinhardt's black diagrams or Klein's monochrome painting-objects. The cut is both a real thing *and* a sign; the black behind it is both a real thing *and* an image. This profoundly paradoxical trickery has an affecting magic of its own. It is a function of Fontana's ironic dandyism, both in his work (which is elegant, extravagant, sometimes ostentatiously and ironically vulgar) and in his 'everyday' appearance (as stylist, gentleman, magician, joker). Even in his studio a black tie and polished shoes seemed *de rigeur*, and, when public occasion demanded, he could affect striped flared trousers, or an outrageously flamboyant fitted

fur coat, a homburg and outsize turn-ups. The continuous performance of Fontana's art-life places him in the line of such seriously antic artists as Marcel Duchamp and Francis Picabia, Klein and Joseph Beuys: it was a means to secure attention to his art, an art crucially necessary to the definitive development of the human imagination.

This artful attention-seeking and exaggeration extended to the oracular opacity and Futuristic rhetoric of his public utterances and manifestos. In his 'Technical Manifesto of Spatialism' (Fontana's own term for his 'programme' of 1952), for example, he proclaimed:

Painted canvas and sculpture no longer make sense … What is needed … is a change in both essence and form. It is necessary to go beyond painting, sculpture and poetry … In praise of this transformation in the nature of man, we abandon the use of known forms of art and move towards the development of an art based upon the unity of space and time.

And in his last interview in 1968 he enquired: 'do you think man will have time to produce art whilst travelling through the universe? He will only have time to travel through space and discover marvellous things, things so beautiful that things here will seem worthless.' For Fontana the entry of an infinite space into art was an aspect of the final stage of art's evolution towards a true multi-dimensional abstraction. The penetration of the support signified, he said, an escape 'from the prison of the flat surface'. The ultimate abstraction would offer an experience of space unlimited by the contingencies of perception: that was the significance of the generic title, *Spatial Concept.* Fontana often remarked, about his own work and that of others, 'It's the *idea* that counts'. For all that, in spite of the visionary idea that informs it, some part of the beauty and truth of his work is to be found in the poignancy of the objects themselves, which carry the evidence of actions physically drastic, circumscribed, earth-bound and time-bound. They have a provisional, all-too-human fullness and fragility.

The paintings of the American artist Agnes Martin have another kind of fragility: the tough fragility of an egg shell. Although they are always made within the strictest constraint of the symmetrical squared grid, or with the even simpler device of regularly spaced parallels of lines or short dashes, they each achieve a marvellous singularity; each is as unique as a moment and as like any other. Martin's art is predicated upon the rhythms of breathing, the invariable regularities of time – day/night, winter/spring/summer/autumn – and yet, with an austere and purely abstract discipline, it *represents*, in the

sense that it is a signifying manifestation of a process of meditation, an activity of the mind and spirit that transcends the physical and the perceptual. Her poetic titles often suggest that an experience of nature might have initiated the purely contemplative process that finds form in the aesthetic construction of the work: *Whispering, Starlight, Ocean Water, White Flower* (1960s); *Mountain Flowers, Fiesta, Grey Geese in Flight* (1980s). An undated note makes clear the relation between their conception and perceptive experience: 'This poem, like the paintings, is not really about nature. It is not what is seen. It is what is *known* forever in the mind.' *Praise* 1985 (fig.65) is typical: its rhythmic repetition, each thick edge-to-edge horizontal alternating with seven barely visible thin stopped lines, induces a contemplative response; the artist's visible procedures provide the 'composition of object' that is the precondition of meditation.

Something very similar is effected by the parallel bars of John McLaughlin's #2 1975 (fig.66), which may be taken to exemplify the meditative tendency of much of the best abstract art in the last thirty years. An American who lived for many years in Japan, McLaughlin was deeply affected in thought and spirit by a specific style of Oriental painting and its implicit philosophy. Like Reinhardt, whom he greatly admired, he sought to find a way to divest painting of all extraneous reference. Following the Japanese brush masters of the fifteenth century whose paintings he had closely studied, he sought to penetrate the appearance of the great manifold of nature, its object forms and the dynamics of their relations, in order to reveal the immaterial emptiness and absolute stillness of the spiritual void behind things. As with the work of Reinhardt and Martin, symmetry and an ordered regularity are necessary to his purposes, not as a conceptual geometry but as an iconic sign: it is not the painting-object that matters so much as the balance of contemplative thought and calmness of spirit it induces in the patient beholder.

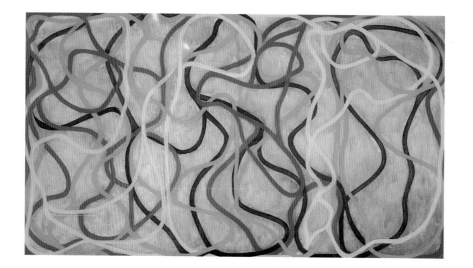

67
Brice Marden

Chinese Dancing
1994–6

Oil on canvas
152.4 × 203.2
(60 × 80)
Paine Webber
Collection

68
Callum Innes

Exposed Painting,
Paynes Grey/Red
Oxide/Asphalt on White
1998

Oil on canvas
230.5 × 224.5
(90¾ × 88¾)
Collection of E.M. and
R.L. Congreve. Courtesy
Frith Street Gallery,
London

69
Peter Joseph

Mute Violet with Blue
1998

Acrylic on cotton duck
141.7 × 150.8
(55¾ × 59¾)
Lisson Gallery, London

Such an art, of apparently inexhaustible diversity but created out of the simplest of abstract components, needs not, as we have seen, be necessarily quasi-geometric or symmetrical, though it will always tend to forms that have graceful poise and simplicity, and may be repeated in endless variations. Among the truly international company of artists whose work shares these qualities and whose art asks for meditative contemplation may be numbered Stephane Bordarier (French); Marcia Hafif, Brice Marden (fig.67), Dorothea Rockburne, Robert Ryman, Richard Tuttle (American); Peter Joseph (fig.69), Maria Lalic (English); Callum Innes (fig.68), Alan Johnston (Scottish); and Sean Shanahan (Irish). Their art is of a kind that makes an appeal to something in our experience that lies beyond words, providing occasion for the realisation that there are things language cannot encompass. The final proposition of Wittgenstein's first great book, *Tractatus Logico-Philosophicus*, written during the First World War and published in 1921, comes at last to mind: 'Whereof one cannot speak, thereof one must be silent.'

POSTSCRIPT: TWO VOICES

The first, that of an artist:

'A painting is made with coloured paint on a surface, and what you see is what you see.' This popular and melancholy cliché is so remote from my own concern. In my experience a painting is not made with colours and paint at all. I don't know what a painting is; who knows what sets off even the desire to paint? It might be things, thoughts, a memory, sensations, which have nothing to do directly with painting itself. They can come from anything and anywhere, a trifle, some detail observed, wondered about and, naturally, from the previous painting. The painting is not on a surface, but on a plane that is imagined. It moves in the mind ... I think the idea of the pleasure of the eye is not merely limited, it isn't even possible. Everything means something. Anything in life or in art, any mark you make has meaning and the only question is, 'what kind of meaning?'

Philip Guston (1978)

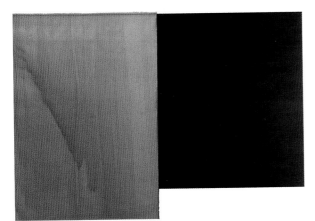

The second, that of a critic:

Abstract art challenges the viewers in a particular way: they are required to look with fresh eyes at pictures that are different. They have to discard old habits, such as the desire to recognise something ... abstract art does not imitate, it represents in a different way. Viewers find no affirmation of themselves in what they see. They are denied the satisfaction of re-encountering a known reality ... One of abstract art's great discoveries is undoubtedly to have made reality's energetic side visible again. It helps us to comprehend that Nature is just as invisible, immaterial and dynamic as it is tangible, concrete and static. The importance of the in-between is rediscovered. The abstract representation of reality is founded on the two-way flow of visual energies.

Gottfried Boehm (1994)

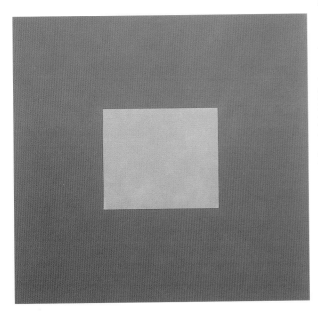

FURTHER READING

What follows is a somewhat personal list. These are publications (in the editions that I have used) that I have found particularly interesting or truly illuminating in the course of writing this book, and which I think are worth taking the time to seek out and consult. A huge literature of books, catalogues and articles has accreted around the subject of abstract art and its practitioners, a great deal of it in line with the conventions of one or another misleading historicism. Much of the current theoretical literature is arcane, repetitive, boring or unreadable.

Abstraction in General

Abstraction: Toward a New Art – Painting 1910–1920, exh. cat. Tate Gallery, London 1980

Barr, Alfred H., *Cubism and Abstract Art,* exh. cat., Museum of Modern Art, New York 1936

Bois, Yve-Alain, *Painting as Model,* Cambridge, Mass./ London 1993

Brùderlin, Markus (ed.), *Foundation Beyeler,* Basel 1997

Chipp, Herschel B. (ed.), *Theories of Modern Art,* London 1968

Fer, Briony, *On Abstract Art,* New Haven and London 1997

Gabo, Naum, J.L. Martin, Ben Nicholson (eds.), *Circle: International Survey of Constructive Art,* London 1937

Gray, Camilla, *The Russian Experiment in Art 1863–1922,* London 1962

Heron, Patrick, *Painter as Critic: Patrick Heron: Selected Writings,* ed. Mel Gooding, London 1998

Lynton, Norbert, *The Story of Modern Art,* Oxford 1980

Moszynska, Anna, *Abstract Art* London 1990

Riley, Bridget, *The Eye's Mind: Bridget Riley Collected Writings 1965–1999,* London 1999

Russian Painting of the Avant Garde, exh. cat., Scottish National Gallery of Modern Art, Edinburgh 1993

Schapiro, Meyer, *Modern Art 19th and 20th Centuries Selected Papers,* vol.2, London 1978

Selz, Peter and Kristine Stiles (eds.), *Theories and Documents of Contemporary Art: A Source Book of Artists' Writings,* Los Angeles and London 1996

The Spiritual in Art: Abstract Painting 1890–1985, exh. cat., Los Angeles Museum of Art, 1986

1 Abstraction and the Invisible
Malevich and Russia

Beeren, W.A.L. and J.M. Joosten, (eds.), *Kazimir Malevich 1878–1935,* exh. cat., Stedelijk Museum, Amsterdam 1989

Malevich, K.S., *Essays on Art* ed. Troels Anderson, 2 vols., London 1968

New Art for a New Era: Malevich's Vision of the Russian Avant-Garde, exh. cat., Barbican Art Gallery, London 1999

Petrova, Evgeniya, et al., *Malevich: Artist and Theoretician,* Paris 1990

Rowell, Margit and Angelica Zander Rudenstine, *Art of the Avant-Garde in Russia: Selections from the George Costakis Collection,* exh. cat., Solomon

R. Guggenheim Museum, New York 1981

Rudenstine, Angelica Zander (ed.), *Russian Avant-Garde Art: The George Costakis Collection,* London 1981

Kandinsky

Grohmann, W., *Wassily Kandinsky,* London 1959

Kandinsky, Wassily, *Concerning the Spiritual in Art,* New York 1977

Lindsay, Kenneth C. and Peter Vergo (eds.), *Complete Writings on Art,* 2 vols., London 1982

Lamaè, Miroslav, *František Kupka,* Prague 1984

Roethel, Hans K. and Jean K. Benjamin, *Kandinsky: Catalogue Raisonné of the Oil-Paintings,* 2 vols., London 1982, 1984

Mondrian

Bois, Yves-Alain, Hans Janssen, Joop Joosten, and Angelica Zander Rudenstine (eds.), *Piet Mondrian 1872–1944,* exh. cat., Little, Brown & Co., New York 1994

Jaffe, Hans L.C., *Mondrian,* London 1969

Mondrian, Piet, *Natural Reality and Abstract Reality: An Essay in Trialogue Form,* New York 1995

2 Abstraction and the Visible
Cubism

Baldessari, Anne, *Picasso and Photography: The Dark Mirror,* Paris 1997

Cooper, Douglas and Gary Tinterow, *The Essential Cubism 1907–1920,* exh. cat., Tate Gallery, London 1983

Dorival, Bernard, *The School of Paris,* London 1962

Cowling, Elizabeth and John Golding, *Picasso: Sculptor/*

Painter, exh. cat., Tate Gallery, London 1994

Rubin, William, *Picasso and Braque: Pioneering Cubism,* exh. cat., Museum of Modern Art, New York 1989

Pure Painting and the New 'Realism'

Apollinaire, Guillaume, *Apollinaire on Art,* London 1972

Léger, Fernand, *Functions of Painting,* London 1973

Léger and Purist Paris, exh. cat., Tate Gallery, London 1970

3 Constructivisms
Tatlin's Dream

Configuration 1910–1940, exh. cat., Annely Juda, London 1981

Dabrowski, Magdalena, *Liubov Popova,* exh. cat., Museum of Modern Art, New York 1991

Dada–Constructivism: The Janus Face of the Twenties, exh. cat., Annely Juda, London 1984

Elliot, David (ed.), *Alexander Rodchenko,* exh. cat., Museum of Modern Art, Oxford 1979

Tatlin's Dream: Russian Suprematist and Constructivist Art 1910–1923, exh. cat., Fischer Fine Art, London 1973

Zhadova, Larissa Alekseevna, *Tatlin,* London 1988

International Constructivism

Bann, Stephen (ed.), *The Tradition of Constructivism ,* London 1974

Dada and Constructivism, exh. cat., Museum of Modern Art, Tokyo 1988

Doesberg, Theo van, *Principles of Neo-Plastic Art,* London 1968

Friedman, Mildred (ed.), *De Stijl: 1917–1931 Visions of Utopia*, Oxford 1982

Jaffe, Hans L.C. (ed.), *De Stijl*, London 1971

Kurt Schwitters, exh. cat., Tate Gallery, London 1985

Kurt Schwitters, exh. cat., Marlborough Fine Art, London 1981

Overy, Paul, *De Stijl*, London 1969

Geometries of the Mind

Gabo, Naum, *Of Divers Arts*, New York 1962

Helms, Dietrich (ed.), *Vordemberge-Gildewart: The Complete Works*, Munich 1990

Kostelanetz, Richard, *Moholy-Nagy*, London 1971

L. Moholy-Nagy, exh. cat., Arts Council of Great Britain / Institute of Contemporary Arts, London 1980

Max Bill / Georges Vantongerloo: A Working Friendship, exh. cat., Annely Juda, London 1996

Naum Gabo: The Constructivist Idea, exh. cat., South Bank Centre, London 1987

Staber, Margit, *Max Bill*, London 1964

Vantongerloo, Georges, *Paintings, Sculptures, Reflections*, New York 1948

4 Post-war Abstractions

Actions in the Arena

Arshile Gorky, exh. cat., Whitechapel Art Gallery, London 1989

Art Since 1945, London 1959 (no editor given; various writers)

Barnett Newman, exh. cat., Tate Gallery, London 1972

Joachimiddes, Christos M. and Norman Rosenthal (eds.), *American Art in the 20th Century: Painting and Sculpture 1913–1993*, exh. cat., Royal Academy of Arts, London 1993

The New American Painting, exh. cat., Tate Gallery, London 1959

Mark Rothko, exh. cat., Tate Gallery, London 1987

Robertson, Bryan, *Jackson Pollock*, London 1960

Rose, Barbara, *American Art since 1900: A Critical History*, London 1967

Varnadoe, Kirk with Pepe Karmel, *Jackson Pollock*, exh. cat., Tate Gallery, London 1999

The Return of Nature

Gooding, Mel, *John Hoyland*, London 1990

Lynton, Norbert, *Ben Nicholson*, London 1993

Nicolas de Staël, exh. cat., Tate Gallery, London 1981

Sutton, Denys, *Nicolas de Staël*, London 1960

Willem de Kooning, exh. cat., Whitney Museum of American Art, New York 1984

Fullness and Emptiness

Ad Reinhardt, exh. cat., Museum of Contemporary Art, Los Angeles / Museum of Modern Art, New York 1991

Fontana, exh. cat., Whitechapel Art Gallery, London 1988

John McLaughlin: Western Modernism Eastern Thought, exh. cat., Laguna Art Museum, Laguna Beach, Calif. 1996

Lucio Fontana, exh. cat., Hayward Gallery, London 1999

Rose, Barbara (ed.), *Art-as-Art: The Selected Writings of Ad Reinhardt*, New York 1975

Sidra Stich, *Yves Klein*, exh. cat., Hayward Gallery, London 1995